# Advance Praise

*"**SARAH EXCAVATES FROM** within hidden caves the bare bones of our misplaced soul purpose, and lays out the tools she uses to piece them back together in easily digestible, heartfelt gold nuggets. She showcases deeply vulnerable accounts of personal triumph over anxiety and pain, so we may see our human experiences as gifts and believe in our own capacity to stand in the light. Whether through her tried and true coaching exercises, her thought-provoking questions, or her Rumi-esque poems, Sarah asks the reader to pause, to spend time with oneself, to reflect on the greater implication of one's healing process, and to take bold action. She stands up for the part of us that we quieted, the one that yearns to be heard and deserves to be awoken.*

*"If you are a dreamer, a healer, or just seeking answers, then buckle up, grab a pen and paper, and start reading this. It's a big 'yes' to yourself."*

   –Asha Eden
   Owner and founder of the Awakening

*"**SARAH KLEINER IS** a shining star in the human potential movement. Her story is a powerful example of how to transmute some of life's toughest challenges*

*into love and highest potential. As a recovering anxiety-ridden, overachieving perfectionist, Sarah's story resonates deeply with me. The insights, tools, and wisdom she shares will inspire deep transformation for anyone who reads this book. Sarah walks the talk and does the deepest work in her own life, which is why she can speak with such integrity and clarity in her writing. She is speaking from experience, and the combination of her sharp intellect, loving heart, and beautiful soul make this book an experience that everyone will greatly benefit from reading."*

    **–Lindsay Sukornyk**
      Founder of Alive + Awake

*"**I HAVE OFTEN** felt like my life had a bigger purpose than the one I was currently settling for working as an RN. For years, I ignored this feeling and told myself that I should be satisfied in the job I had…that being a nurse should be enough…but, frankly, it just wasn't. After reading* Soul Nudge, *I now understand that that gut feeling I had stifled for years was never meant to go away, but to be a driving force in making a bigger impact in the world and creating the life I've always dreamed of. This book not only gave me tangible steps on how to move forward with starting my business but also taught me how to listen to my intuition, overcome inevitable obstacles, and really tune into and be clear on what my heart desires. If you are needing a soul pep talk along with ways to put one entrepreneurial foot in front of the other, this book should be the place you start!"*

    **–Shelby Kurz**
      Founder of Unbound Nurse Coaching

# Soul Nudge

# Soul Nudge

## Uncovering What You're Meant to Create

BY SARAH KLEINER

Un-Settling Books
Boulder, Colorado USA

Copyright © Sarah Kleiner, 2018

All rights reserved.

No part of this publication may be reproduced or transmitted in any form or by any means, mechanical or electronic, including photocopying or recording, or by any information storage and retrieval system, or transmitted by email without permission in writing from the author. Reviewers may quote brief passages in reviews. For permissions, contact Sarah Kleiner at sarah@sarahkleiner.com.

Neither the author nor the publisher assumes any responsibility for errors, omissions, or contrary interpretations of the subject matter herein. Any perceived slight of any individual or organization is purely unintentional.

Cover Design: Sarah Kleiner
Cover Implementation & Content Design: Sally Wright Day
Editing: Maggie McReynolds
Author's photo courtesy of Atley Marks

ISBN: 978-0-578-53072-7

# Dedication

This book is dedicated to those closest to me,
who poured love into my heart
when I needed it the most.
My husband, who has been by my side
for this wild ride.
My mom, who planted so many of the seeds
that evolved into my business
and my book.
And my dad's spirit, who has been
showing me so many lessons along the way.

*SOUL NUDGE: UNCOVERING WHAT YOU'RE MEANT TO CREATE*

# Contents

Introduction  xi

    Chapter 1: Figuring It Out  1
    Chapter 2: Where Did It All Start?  5
    Chapter 3: Allow It to Unfold  11
    Chapter 4: The Day You Created  15
    Chapter 5: Let in Your Vision  21
    Chapter 6: Building a Relationship with Your Soul  27
    Chapter 7: You Say You Want Answers  33
    Chapter 8: Clearing the Path  37
    Chapter 9: Give Yourself Some Credit  43
    Chapter 10: Growing Pains  47
    Chapter 11: Where Can You Start?  53
    Chapter 12: Overwhelmed by All the Choices?  59
    Chapter 13: Owning the Path You're Meant to Take  65
    Chapter 14: What Comes After Yes?  71
    Chapter 15: You Actually Are Ready  77
    Chapter 16: Your Path to Leadership  81
    Chapter 17: What Happens After the Leap?  89
    Chapter 18: Things Will Get in Your Way…Do It Anyway  93
    Chapter 19: It's Meant to Feel Messy  99
    Chapter 20: Let It Keep Growing  105
    Chapter 21: Your Time to Come Alive  111
    Chapter 22: The Universe Is Listening  117
    Chapter 23: Keep Expanding Your Toolkit  123
    Chapter 24: Don't Be Surprised If Resistance Shows Up  129
    Chapter 25: The Universe Is on Your Side  133
    Chapter 26: That Time I Called in All the Ancestors  137
    Chapter 27: Are You Appreciating the Mountain?  147
    Chapter 28: Your Dreams Are Not an Experiment  151

Acknowledgments  155
Resources  159
About the Author  161
Just For You!  163

*SOUL NUDGE: UNCOVERING WHAT YOU'RE MEANT TO CREATE*

# Introduction

Ever since I was five, I knew I was meant to write a book. It took me a while to figure out what the book would even be about. Even if the ideas started flowing, it was a "five years from now" dream. That's how a lot of dreams start, right? You'll start a business in five years. Write a book in five years. Quit the job you don't love in five years. For me, it was the perfect timeframe—soon enough that it could happen, but far enough out that I was off the hook for taking action. I could push that thought aside for later.

I'll bet you can already think of some "five years from now" dreams in your life too. Maybe you've got one in mind right now. Maybe it's tucked away on the list of ideas stored in a note on your phone. Maybe you've said it once or twice to a close friend. Maybe your dream is on your intentions list every New Year's Eve. Maybe you journal on it all the time.

You might not know all the details yet, but ideas pop

into your head that excite you and, likely, terrify you. There are things on that list you have no idea how to make happen, and, honestly, you aren't even completely sure what idea you're meant to focus on. Usually, you push it all aside with the thought, "I'll come back to it…" you know, five years from now.

This book exists because I stopped telling myself the "five years from now" story and decided to actually try some things on my idea list. I went on a journey to explore what I really wanted, and got serious about making it happen. I let go of the stories that I wasn't ready, or that now wasn't the time. I started taking action, even if they were small actions to begin with, and each step took me to some pretty amazing places. Those places gave me wild stories to tell, deep lessons to share, and experiences I realized other people needed to hear.

I'm writing this book so it finds the people who need it. So it finds you, the woman who has been through some challenging times in life already. You've seen that life is short. That unexpected things can happen. That we can't take this life for granted. You have a heart of gold, and you want to make a difference. You're ready to heal, both yourself and others. You're ready to make some of those "five years from now" dreams a reality. You're ready to acknowledge there is another way to move through life. And you're looking for a little bit more of the how. How to heal. How to open up. How to create. How to figure out which steps to take next.

Throughout this book, I'll be wearing my heart on my sleeve. Sharing my stories, my healing, and my tools. I dive into things I did to help heal my nervous system and my anxiety, and to get to know the authentic me. I share what helped me step up as a leader and an entrepreneur. Not because I have any pre-conceived notion that your story looks just like mine, but because through each word, each sentence, and each chapter, I hope you see a bit of you. Maybe it's a bit of you that you're trying to grow—a future version of you that you're excited to become. Maybe it's a bit of you that you've locked out for far too long, and need to reclaim.

It's no accident you picked up this book. It's no accident our souls are connecting. So as we dive in, I want to honor you. I see your heart. I see your drive. I see your deep passion for making the world a better place. And I honor the fact that, even for just this moment in time, I get to help you take a step forward on your journey.

You're about to embark on a process of uncovering the authentic you.

*SOUL NUDGE: UNCOVERING WHAT YOU'RE MEANT TO CREATE*

CHAPTER 1

# Figuring It Out

Does some of this sound familiar?

You're eager and, truthfully, a little impatient to figure it all out: your purpose, your passion, and how you can help the world. You want to feel clear, confident, and free. You want to create a life that truly feels good to you, one where you do the things you love and feel lit up every day.

You've been searching for work that you feel passionate about, something that feels fulfilling. You've probably tried a few different jobs and done volunteer work, and while you've been good at those jobs, they just seemed to bring you more clarity on what you don't want. At the end of the day, you're left wondering what is really going to make you happy.

You are tired of dealing with overwhelm, stress, anxiety, and your body feeling exhausted. You're ready to feel like your life is completely in alignment. You daydream about more travel, but while vacations and disconnecting from your phone and social media feel amazing, you know the answer isn't shutting out the problem or traveling for the next five years to avoid deciding what to do next. There's a next step just waiting to reveal itself. What is it?

You're not afraid of hard work. You're the type who loves to work toward big goals, whether it's a promotion at work, personal development events, or starting to work out more. You keep growing in so many ways. You're constantly in search of what will make your life, your body, and your mind feel better.

Ideas are always popping into your head. It's exciting, but also overwhelming. It feels like either you have no idea what you're meant to do next, or that there are 25 options all grasping for your attention. You're realizing that you need to pick something—take some kind of action—but you want to know where to focus and what's really meant for you. If this phase of your life were a chapter in a book, it would probably be titled, "Figuring It Out."

And so, this chapter actually is.

I've been in your shoes. I know how many emotions come up when you want to connect the dots, and put together the puzzle pieces. You're ready to welcome the things meant for you and to feel the peace and calm of knowing you're on the right path. I've felt the same doubt, frustration, curiosity, hopelessness, anger, and excitement. The words in this book could easily be pages torn out from my journal.

Know this: each step and each moment is leading you

where you're meant to be. Every wish you've made and every dream you've had is a seed you've planted that will grow into so much more. There's an intention inside of you that's ready to be acknowledged, seen, and heard.

It's clear to me now that I set my intention far before I knew I wanted to run a business, or even had a clear picture of how I was going to help other people. When I scroll through the notes section of my phone, it seems obvious what fire was motivating me. I didn't know where the path was leading, but I felt deeply called to provide even just a touch of hope, inspiration, or motivation to others.

That simple intention has led to a business, retreats, a book, and so much more.

You have the root of that intention already, even if you can't see it yet. It's time to grow.

*We're all like raindrops,*
*Not sure where we'll end up.*
*Continually feeling like we're falling from the sky.*

*Deep inside,*
*There's a knowing.*
*Knowing it's for a reason.*
*Knowing we have a purpose.*

*We're just waiting for the flowers to bloom,*
*So we'll know*
*We did our job.*

*SOUL NUDGE: UNCOVERING WHAT YOU'RE MEANT TO CREATE*

CHAPTER 2

# Where Did It All Start?

To really understand where you're going, we also have to acknowledge where you've come from. What key moments brought you to where you are today?

I had a history of anxiety growing up. Panic attacks. Sweaty palms. Blushing from head to toe. Calling in sick to sex ed class for fear I'd blush when they talked about pregnancy (even though I most certainly wasn't pregnant). Looking up at a clock during a test and blushing, as anxiety set in that even just looking up from my paper would make the teacher think I was cheating.

There were constant worries running through my head. My thoughts raced. During medical examinations, it was common for my doctors to ask, "Is this a rash?" when looking at my beet-red blush, or to observe, "You're running really hot and a little sweaty—is everything okay?" Of course, people calling it out only made it worse.

On one occasion, a doctor actually prescribed me anti-anxiety medications. I walked away from the appointment feeling a little unsettled. Something felt off about taking them. As much as it was comforting to have the option, it felt like I'd be numbing a part of myself. Like I wouldn't fully be myself. Like I'd be masking the problem instead of fixing it.

I never ended up taking those pills, and I started to get more and more determined to find another way to deal with my anxiety.

Truthfully, that meant some tough moments. I remember many days of coming home bawling after work because my anxiety, combined with the high pressure of a job in crisis communications, had me so strung out. I was working at a public relations agency supporting a Fortune 500 company in privacy, security, and reliability issues. We were the go-to team when things went wrong and the company had to tell the public about it. We had a war room. We were on-call nights, weekends, and holidays. Usually, we were making decisions at an insanely fast pace. My anxious tendencies made me extremely good at the job, because the details were screaming in my mind and the worries made me extremely proactive. Yet it was exhausting. The stress was feeding the flames of worry in my brain.

I remember being on call on New Year's Eve when a crisis came in, and I was meant to be the lead. It was a big one that had captured the attention of the CEO, and I was being asked to make decisions incredibly quickly. I managed to get the tasks done and then, sitting on my bed,

## Chapter 2: Where Did It All Start?

I broke down crying with fear, worry, and stress pouring out of me. During those moments, I'd wonder how in the world I'd gotten to this place.

I thought I'd done everything right. I loved to write and tell stories, so I had studied journalism and had been on the school paper from the ninth grade through my senior year of college. I loved feature stories about inspirational individuals who overcame crazy challenges and were doing incredible things. I was convinced my role in life was to become a journalist for a big-time newspaper and tell the stories of the hidden heroes.

I was always a hard worker, and I'd gotten good grades in school. I liked to keep my options open, and worked hard just so I'd have more choices. Yet, when it came to decision time, I usually overthought it. Pros and cons lists. Lots of worrying. In the end, I always felt unsure.

I was in college at the height of the "death of journalism." Online magazines and newspapers were starting to pop up, and everyone was saying print journalism was a dying field. The online world was still incredibly uncertain, and most universities weren't teaching what students needed to prepare for the real world. I got scared. I wanted a job right out of school so I could be financially independent and start creating the life I'd always imagined. So halfway through college, I switched majors to public relations. It was a growing field with tons of job prospects. I told myself I would still be telling stories and working with people, just in a slightly different way.

I promised myself I'd have a job before walking in college graduation, and sure enough, I did. I didn't know about the Law of Attraction at the time, but that was my first example of having an intention, trusting the Universe, and manifesting something. There wasn't a doubt in my mind that I'd have a job before I walked at graduation. I set the intention and showed the Universe how serious I was as I put in countless hours in informational interviews and applications. In the end I had the manifestation to show for it. Again, it felt like I was doing everything right. I had my own apartment and a decent-paying job within a month of graduating from college.

A few years into that job, things just weren't feeling right. I was anxious and stressed, and nothing actually felt fun. I would do "fun" activities, but it didn't feel like I was fully enjoying them. I was doing things I thought would feel good—shopping, nice dinners, occasional vacations—but I never felt truly happy. It was taking a toll on my body, too, with back pain, neck pain, and migraines.

I started looking for solutions to help my physical health. Yoga and different types of massages were the easiest place to start. My brain thought that was all I needed, but soon the people I met in those spaces were introducing me to authors and speakers talking about things I found myself oddly curious about. I started reading books about having a purpose in life, what really creates happiness, and the power of the mind. The recommended reading from those authors and speakers, led me to spiritual books, ones talking about your soul choosing to show up on Earth and the Law of Attraction. I wasn't quite sure what to think of it all, but I was open to learning.

All of this was unfolding because my anxiety led me

to a place where I had to figure out how to feel better. My body felt off, and my emotions were all mixed up (and in retrospect, there were so many emotions I wasn't even feeling at the time). My life seemed just fine, but I wasn't happy. I was snapping at the people I loved. Nothing felt fun. I felt depressed, and was having a harder and harder time snapping out of it.

What I can see now is this mission to heal myself, and fix what wasn't working in my own life, would lead to a deep desire to help others. My anxiety led me to personal development. To different types of alternative healing. To yoga. And ultimately, to starting my own business.

The details of my story might not be an exact match for the details of yours, but it's equally as important that you go on this journey of self-discovery. Those feelings of discomfort and dissatisfaction that you've felt bubbling up only go away when you commit to moving forward. You get to decide when you truly open up to what the Universe is trying to tell you, and how to move forward with willingness and an open heart.

What I didn't realize until much later is that each moment of my life has been a breadcrumb. Each time it felt like things were a mess and I didn't know how to fix it, my answers were actually right in front of me.

You doing this work is incredibly important, not just to you, but to the rest of the world. It matters that you feel happy, lit up, on fire, and that you are loving your life. In some way, you are here to make a difference. Making a difference doesn't need to be solving world hunger (although you can definitely contribute to this effort!). It can mean being the happiest interior designer the world has ever seen. It can mean having slow mornings where you take care of yourself so you have more love to give your friends and family. Your happiness, your joy, and your love will spread to others and make a difference.

I feel the pleading from the Earth. She needs more kindness. More happy people. More love in the world. More light. So if it's your art, your healing, your coaching—whatever feels light and exciting in your heart—please take it seriously. Please do it. Please let that light expand in as many ways as you can. The world needs your energy, love, and happiness to spread as much as possible.

When I felt that last paragraph come through, I became very emotional. A few tears hit the page. Because I can feel the energy of the souls waiting for you. The ones in pain who need your light, your guidance, and your gifts in some way. The ones who will benefit from your example of living a life that you truly love. They need you, and are the reason you're here to step up.

This book is here to serve as a guide. To give you some of the tools you need so you aren't on this path alone. There's something that brought you to this moment, to this book, and we're about to connect the dots to learn what that is.

CHAPTER 3

# Allow It to Unfold

We're on a mission to understand what's next for you. To understand what your soul is saying, where your intuition is pointing you, and what next steps you're meant to take.

That's a big undertaking, right?

My intention in sharing some deeply raw parts of my story is to unlock those parts in you. As I lay my heart on the line, my journey of blooming, finding myself, listening to my soul, and setting myself free might touch something in you. You might see yourself in the people-pleasing version of me, the anxiety-ridden girl learning to take risks, or the dreamer tired of waiting for "one day." I hope it stirs up a part of you that has been yearning to be seen.

I hope my stories make you think about the path in life you really want to take. I hope you see some of your own frustrations, sadness, and fears, and also feel the hope, potential, and magic that I know is possible for you.

In this space, in this book, we get to break it down step by step. Because truthfully, when you set the ambiguous goal to "figure it out," your brain can get in the way. A lot.

We'll go through the tools you'll need to tune into your inner knowing. We'll help you build a practice so that when you sit quietly for a few minutes, you'll feel something shift in your body. You'll feel a bit more trust, and a knowing that there's more to come. It's not just a feeling of calm because you've slowed down in the moment, it's a deep and grounded calm from knowing you're on the right path. You're taking steps forward. You are being guided, directed, led to exactly where you need to go.

You'll trust that peaceful feeling. Trust exactly where you are in this moment. Throughout this book, we're going to allow your journey to unfold. We'll go through a process that helps you feel what your heart is trying to tell you, build a relationship with your soul and your intuition, paint a picture of what your vision is, and understand what steps forward you're meant to take.

It's time to dive in.

*With the sky on fire.*
*And tea in my hand.*
*It's fitting.*
*The thoughts racing in our minds.*
*But the peace in our hands.*
*We get to appreciate the beauty of both.*
*And know, at the end of the day,*

*It's all fleeting. It's just for this moment.*

*Sometimes that's a relief,*

*But usually I feel anxiety.*

*I like this moment. I like this place. What's to come?*

*And I remind myself.*

*There's more goodness to come.*

*Knowing that is what got me here in the first place.*

CHAPTER 4

# The Day You Created

It can be a freeing and also terrifying moment when you realize things in your life might need to change. Maybe the job isn't working. Maybe you don't love the city you're in. Maybe it feels like life keeps putting speed bumps in the road, and you don't know why.

For me, it all started with that corporate job in crisis communications. It was a job I'd worked hard to get. My whole life I had prioritized whatever needed to happen to make me "successful" by other people's standards. I was a great student, got into top colleges, graduated in three years instead of four, and had an internship at a top PR agency secured before I even got my diploma. I moved up in the professional world quickly, always keeping in mind my long-term goals. I figured out what I was good at and pursued that persistently, with success my unwavering goal. Yet soon into my career, when I found myself wondering about the next step, I noticed that the prospect of the next promotion, or even the two after that, didn't feel all that satisfying.

Working at a corporate job was what I thought I "should" do. I don't think I really understood what it meant to be in that world. I just found the steady, decently large paycheck appealing, and it made me feel intelligent and successful to have the job title and be working my way up the ladder. Honestly, most of my life was doing what I "should" do to feel successful, to feel smart, to feel like I was doing life in the "right" way. I wanted to prove to everyone that I was as smart, determined, and capable as they thought I was. I wanted what they wanted for me: to make a name for myself. But in doing so, I had taken on many definitions of success that weren't my own.

Noticing that this wasn't actually what I wanted was revolutionary for me. These things I thought I wanted—and that I'd worked so hard for—weren't making me happy. And that brought up a lot of really uncomfortable truths.

Once I was willing to look, I saw that living right next door to the city I'd grown up in wasn't working for me. Overachieving wasn't working for me. I was good and well-practiced at working hard, but I was also burning out at an incredibly fast rate. It kept eating at me that all that effort didn't feel like it was making an impact—certainly not one that mattered to me.

Things were going to have to change, and that was deeply uncomfortable for me. I'd had a complicated relationship with change since childhood, when my father had a serious accident that meant change had been more or less thrust on me and my family. I'd learned that I might not be able to control my loved ones' health, if friends moved away, or if I needed to transfer schools, but I could control how hard I worked, how many colleges I applied to, and my test scores.

I couldn't control change, and that scared me. I'd learned to appreciate the people and things around me, but that also made it very difficult to leave them, regardless of whether that departure was voluntary or not.

There was also some guilt when stepping out from what was "safe," what I "should do." I usually knew what people wanted me to do—what they found logical or reasonable; what wouldn't stress them out or make them worry. And if I picked something that the people around me didn't like, a part of me felt guilty because I was perfectly capable of doing what they wanted. I knew how, and I could make it happen. I just didn't.

I lived that way for a long time, trying to impress other people and make them happy. I could almost always do it, but it was exhausting. In order to pull it off, I'd had to hide behind a mask almost my whole life—covered up by the story "I'm fine."

I didn't really know I was lying. I actually thought I was fine, that I had it handled. I was the responsible one. The one who took care of others. The one who figured out her own shit so other people didn't have to deal with it.

I was fine after my dad was hit by a car when I was eight years old. I was fine in college while conquering the goal of graduating in three years instead of four and working three different internships to ensure I had a job by the time I graduated. I was fine at my first job, getting promoted three times in two years and taking on more responsibility and stress than my body knew what to do with.

Oh yeah, I was fine.

I had it handled.

I knew how to be strong.

Now the Universe was asking me to take off the mask and take my walls down. To acknowledge that I didn't have to be fully broken for things to need to change. That I was able to ask for more, to ask for better, and that was truly okay.

It sounds so simple, right? But when you've been running away from your feelings for a long time, it can feel really complicated.

When you sit with it and really think about it, where have you been saying things are "fine"? What areas in your life do you allow others to believe you're happy, when maybe deep down you've been curious about life looking a little different? What are your "shoulds"? "Should" you save up more money before you take the trip? Have more experience at the job before your start your own business? Hang on until the next promotion because things will get better then?

Where have you been saying things are "fine," when really your heart is asking for an upgrade?

A friend helped me embrace change by asking me to picture what my ideal day actually was. He had me write it out: What did my perfect day look like? Specifically, he asked me to focus on an ideal day that was happening after I'd already spent a year traveling, on vacation, truly relaxing. Basically, what the "average" day would look like, but in my ideal world. For me, that day involved things like sleeping in, getting time to relax in the morning with some tea or coffee, lots of snuggles with my cats, going for a run or doing yoga, getting outside to explore, writing on the beach with the sun on my face, and doing work that I felt proud of, work I knew was truly helping the world.

When I first wrote out that ideal day, it felt like an imaginary world. It was so different than my current reality at that point, and writing about it felt like I was just dreaming. But there was a little voice in my head that kept asking me what I was truly working for if not this ideal day. Why did I get up early for work? Why did I pour my heart and soul into my corporate job? Why did I spend all my time and energy doing things that weren't getting me any closer to making this dream day a reality?

At first I tried to push that little voice away. I would tell myself that one day, the "right" opportunity would come around, or that my job was still a good step for now, or that I was young and had lots of time to figure it out. But that little voice kept getting louder over time, until I realized something had to change.

Take a minute to write out what an ideal day looks like for you. Get super specific. Where do you wake up? What makes you smile? What brings you joy? What's most meaningful in your day? If there are details that aren't clear, it's fine. Stick with what you do know. Don't worry about how it would all come about. Just trust for a moment that you'll soon know the steps that will make it actually possible.

This will be one of a few different times you'll be writing things down throughout this book, so take this moment to either start a note in your phone, or to go to a couple of blank pages in your journal. All these moments will add up, so make sure you keep it all in one place. If you'd prefer to keep reading and catch up with these writing prompts later, you'll find them all linked at the back of the book.

*We run in circles,*

*Hoping that one day, we'll be enough.*

*Smart enough.*

*Successful enough.*

*Popular enough.*

*Pretty enough.*

*But enough…for who?*

*What if we made our own rules?*

*What if we decided what really matters?*

*It would truly be a revolution.*

*But the kind where we are all too busy making our own lives awesome, leaving no time to judge others.*

CHAPTER 5

# Let in Your Vision

There are probably a lot of questions racing around in your head. It feels like there's so much yet to unfold! And yet there also are some answers ready to be heard, answers that are right on the tip of your tongue.

When you think about what's out of alignment in your life right now, what's the first thought that comes to your head? What's the first place energy wants to flow?

Go with the first thing that comes to mind. Write it down in your phone or journal. Oftentimes we make this overly complicated, when in fact our first answer can show so much.

As my journey started unfolding, an answer to my misalignment came bubbling up no matter how much I wanted to deny it. It came through like a scream in my head while I was on a walk with my then-fiancé (now my husband).

We were taking a walk in the park after work. We lived in a nice part of town and had recently upgraded from the small, old studio we snagged after college to a much bigger, beautiful apartment. I was still working in crisis communications, and my husband had a job at a start-up in Seattle. We lived near family, and it all made so much sense.

Yet what came out of my mouth was: "We have to get OUT of here!!!!"

There it was. This desperate need for things to change. This hugely inconvenient request, considering that both of our families lived in the area and we had good jobs, a nice apartment, and a life that had come together quite nicely exactly where we were. I wasn't necessarily sure we'd live there forever…but I also didn't feel completely sure that it was the right time to move.

I'd gotten that tap on my shoulder, though. And it wasn't exactly a quiet one.

I reminded myself that I couldn't spend every day until I was 85 doing the same thing, making the same choice, living in the same city, doing the same job, without looking back and regretting it. I knew that I had to choose something different. I knew there needed to be more chapters to my story. Even if it turned out to be a mistake, making a change made me feel like I was living life.

I started letting in the idea of moving.

That led to considering options of where to relocate. My fiancé and I picked five cities that we'd love to live in and that felt exciting (although, admittedly, still pretty terrifying to me). I started applying for jobs in PR in those areas, since that felt like the easiest way to make the transition. Within a month, I had a job offer at a different PR firm. We were officially moving to San Francisco.

As soon as there were actual details, like where and how, the emotions came on strong. I felt guilty leaving family behind. I felt scared to find a new place and unsure if I was making the right decision. It felt hard to honor my alignment and my needs when nothing was actually wrong with the current reality. There was this constant, nagging worry: Should I really risk giving up what I had? Maybe I was being ungrateful. Maybe I'd actually gone crazy.

Looking back, the thing I wish I could've told that version of me is how life-changing her choice would be. How deeply proud she should be for saying yes to that voice, the one asking to go in a new direction.

You've likely already made some decision in your life that's felt like this. You've honored a soul nudge in some way. Maybe it was changing jobs the first time. Maybe it was taking a solo weekend trip. Maybe it was moving to a new place for college, or after college. Maybe it was even quitting a soul-sucking job. You had a moment of that voice yelling at you, and you made the choice to pick what would likely make you happy in the long run.

So in this moment, what do you know? The next step might not be as big as moving or quitting your job. It could be a thought about what you're craving and what feelings you want more of. What do you know about what you want to create? What do you know about what your next step is? What do you know about what you're wanting in life?

To clarify, I'm not saying you have to pack up all your

belongings and move to discover what you're really meant to do in life. What it really takes is a fresh perspective. What if you viewed every single thing in your life as optional? What if literally nothing was required, and you had a completely blank slate? What would you truly want to do?

I know, your brain is probably already protesting, telling you that you need that job, or that there's no way you can give up that responsibility. Let me calm your thoughts just a bit by saying I'm not asking you to throw everything out. What I want you to consider is that there are parts of your vision you really do know. When you think about what to write on your blank slate, ask yourself: What do you know about how you want to help people? About how you'd spend your time? About what topics you'd want to learn about, the things you'd want to share?

Sometimes the options can feel overwhelming. When I started exploring this, I kept following one seemingly "random" thought after another. I found I knew some things. Deep down inside, I knew I wanted to be an entrepreneur "someday." I knew loved yoga communities. I knew that nature was always my happy place. I loved to write.

I started with these simple truths, and took small actions to put time and energy into what I knew. Since I loved yoga, it was time for more yoga classes. Since I wanted to be an entrepreneur at some point, it made sense to start exploring personal development that would get me ready for that change, and entrepreneur communities to start to learn how that big shift might happen.

When you accept that your thoughts aren't random,

you start to open up the possibilities. So notice what excites you. Notice the idea that pops into your head and makes you smile or makes your heart feel lighter. You don't need to know where it's leading or how it will evolve, and you don't have to worry about if it makes "sense" in this moment. Watch what you daydream as you walk through nature, or where your thoughts go when you sit to meditate. When you go to bed at night, what do you wish the next day would look like? When you wake up in the morning and check your calendar, what do you want to see on it this week? This month? Even this year?

Write down a list of what your vision is, in this moment. Nothing is too small, too vague, or too crazy. What do you know? What has been tapping you on the shoulder? What are the parts you do feel certain of, even if the rest is still coming together? Is there an idea you've been afraid to say out loud? A thought that feels meant for five years from now? In this moment, put your pen to paper or open the notes section of your phone, and let it all be seen and heard.

The processing of uncovering who you are and what you're here for feels like remembering. It's uncovering puzzle pieces that don't always make sense right away, but will fit together over time. It's believing in yourself even when no one else can see the vision yet, and when the path doesn't make any sense.

CHAPTER 6

# Building a Relationship with Your Soul

*I* didn't realize at the time that moving was me following a soul nudge. Those times you've said yes to trying something new, to taking a risk, to following your heart, you were also following these nudges. It's that voice, or feeling, that taps you on the shoulder every so often.

Think about those times where a thought has popped into your head that felt really good. Maybe it was when you were sitting inside, working, and you looked out the window and thought about going for a walk. It could have been a dinner idea that sounded really amazing and you lit up inside, even just a little, as you thought about it.

There can be big soul nudges, like changing jobs or moving, and small ones that show you what you're craving in this moment. You've likely taken action on these feelings without knowing it, even if the concept feels new or completely foreign.

Already, as you've been writing some of these lists, you might have noticed what feels like a little voice in the back of your head. It's stored where your thoughts are, but it feels just slightly different than a normal thought. It doesn't have the worry or stress of the thoughts in the forefront of your mind. It's a little voice that sometimes feels quiet, like a whisper, and usually has some excitement to it. Sometimes you really have to hunt for it, and sometimes the idea pops into your head loud and clear. Often times it can be pushed aside all too easily and ignored.

There's so much power in that first instinct. I want you to keep an eye on what answer pops up first, in the 30 seconds after you ask yourself a question. Notice the raw, unfiltered feeling that arises. That's your soul, also called your intuition or your inner voice—and it's ready to be heard.

As we grow up, we're not really taught much about that voice. At most, we're told that we always know what's right, somewhere deep down. That can also be the most frustrating answer ever when you're trying to make a decision and honestly feel like you have no idea what you're meant to do.

Recognizing that inner voice takes practice. So for a moment, I want you to close your eyes. Put your hand on your heart. Take a few deep breaths. Now ask yourself: "What do I want to do later today?" Notice the first idea that pops into your head. Take note of how it feels in your heart. Oftentimes there's a lightness, a feeling of excitement. It might even feel like relief.

## Chapter 6: Building a Relationship with Your Soul

Then, notice how quickly other thoughts swoop into your head. You might have initially answered something like, "Curl up in bed and read a book," but then your brain thought of the dirty dishes or the work piling up in your email. Notice how those thoughts feel in your body and in your heart. There's likely a little tightness, maybe some heaviness. Your body might feel a bit more constricted.

It's a very subtle difference. The key here is to keep checking in with your body, over and over again. To keep making space to ask your soul questions, and hear the answers. Over time, finding and hearing that inner voice becomes more of a natural instinct. Your instinct becomes easier to discern.

The other part of this process, and something not enough people talk about, is how many layers of fear, resistance, and other people's stories can get piled on top of that little light in your soul. Sometimes the fear feels like little scribbles being colored all over your heart. It's the nerves, the worry, maybe even the anxiety. The first step is to feel it and allow every feeling that's present in your body to be seen and heard. What's the thought causing the most fear? What's the worst case scenario? What worry is your body reacting to? Spend time checking in with your body to understand what's coming up, versus pushing it all aside. Our communication with ourselves gets muddled when we ignore what's actually happening in the hope that we can force ourselves to feel how we "should," to "think rationally," or "be realistic."

Instead, open up to hearing it all, and then start to breathe deeply into the areas where you feel fear. Breathe into your heart, which might be racing at the idea of doing something new. Breathe into your stomach, which might be tight at the idea that you might be taking a risk, that there's a chance you could fail. Then, picture what's under that. A mentor once told me that fear is excitement without the breath. So if you breathe, and picture what's under the scribbles, what's there? Taking time to breathe, to meditate, and to check in with your body is so important. It's about really making space to listen on a deep level.

At first, until you practice listening to it, the voice can get muffled pretty easily. Fear can be like a big blanket, making it impossible to see or feel what's under it. The most important thing to know is if you set the intention to listen, and make space for doing so, you will hear and see what you're meant to.

The other key thing to realize is that this voice eventually finds a way to be noticed, no matter what. Life just feels a lot better when you acknowledge it earlier in the process, and love what it's trying to tell you.

I tried suppressing the voice, but it eventually rose up to be seen in the form of meltdowns. I'd get home from my corporate job, exhausted and in tears, and tell my husband that I just couldn't do it anymore. Blurting out, "I just need out of here," was certainly an example as well.

During gentler times, I was able to journal about it, hear it while talking with a friend, or have an idea during a walk in the park.

There are even times where you might flat-out say no to the soul nudge. As I was starting to get serious about building my business, I crossed paths with a coach who was in the same community of online entrepreneurs. She had written a book, traveled the world, and was doing work I found inspiring. I felt compelled to ask for an hour of her time to ask what felt like a million questions about how she got to that point in her journey and career. As we talked about what I was creating, she told me that maybe instead of the event planning business I was so convinced was my path, I was actually meant to be a coach.

I actually laughed.

It certainly wasn't by accident I was led to ask for a conversation with this person. It wasn't by accident that she immediately felt the nudge to bring up this new direction for my work. Yet despite all these things lining up, I struggled to even entertain the idea of coaching at the time.

So understand that the voice might not make sense to you at first. When I first started really listening, I was drawn to spiritual books without knowing if I truly believed the theories they talked about. I felt the urge to move when I'd never lived in a different state from my family. I started a blog even while terrified that someone I knew would read it. I wasn't ready to explain or defend what I was learning and feeling.

We don't need to know the whole picture. Most times, we won't. The key is to keep trusting that voice, and that becomes easier the more and more you practice.

Right now, take time to check in with what your body is feeling. Write down what you're craving, what your soul is calling for, and also how that feels in your body. If you feel blocked, write that down too. Call out the thoughts and feelings that do come up, knowing that acknowledging them is the first step in changing them.

Another way to tune in is to pull out a journal and write "the truth is..." and see what comes up after. I assign this prompt to my clients all the time. When you write out "the truth is..." you give yourself permission to let it all come up: the feelings, the worries, the excitement, and the fears. It takes away the layer of what you should be thinking or feeling, and lets you dive deeper into what your body is really feeling.

Let it all out.

CHAPTER 7

# You Say You Want Answers

While listening to one of many podcasts and Facebook videos I turned to during the commute to my corporate job, I heard the question, "How many minutes a day do you think you listen to your own thoughts?"

At first, I was incredibly confident I'd ace that answer. Did they know how loud my thoughts were? The constant questioning, worry, planning, and preparing? My thoughts were taking over! But then, the question was phrased slightly differently.

"No really…how many minutes a day do you listen to only your own thoughts? No music, no podcasts, no videos. No reading other people's posts or articles. Just your own thoughts."

At that time, I spent most of my morning commute listening to music. I spent the day at work reading emails or scrolling my phone. On the way home, I'd listen to a podcast or an audio book. I'd get home and read, watch TV, or hang out with friends. I spent all my time with other people's thoughts.

That really, deeply stuck with me. We have all these questions: What am I meant to do? What's the next step? What's my path? What's my purpose? Where am I going? Why did it happen? Yet we aren't listening for a single answer. How are we supposed to know what we want when we aren't even ready to hear what we have to say?

This is where meditation started for me. It wasn't even with the goal of a quiet mind. It was truly just leaving space for my thoughts. Even if I sat and let thoughts fly by like clouds for 15 minutes, at least it was my time. It was time with my thoughts, my worries, and my feelings.

I hear from many of my clients that they struggle with meditation. They don't do it, they do it wrong, their thoughts are too loud, or they've never really liked it. Maybe what they've said sounds familiar. If so, I want to challenge you to start simply. Start with a 15-minute timer and some relaxing music in the background. Make space for yourself, even if the whole time you're thinking, "Oh, shit, I'm late for work. I need to shower. The dishes are dirty …" Make space, even for that. Notice that you feel too busy, or feel too rushed, or that worries keep popping into your head. Instead of trying to quiet the thoughts, use the space to just listen.

I started meditating for just 10 minutes in the morning before work. Sometimes I spent the whole time worrying that I would miss the train. But I still made time for it, and my practice grew from there, from 10 minutes to 15 and then 20. I started simply by taking time to think, and time to notice. I would usually journal afterward about what thoughts had come up. Soon, as I kept up the habit, I was able to focus on my breath: focusing on the inhale and then the exhale.

For this week, add at least 10 minutes of daily meditation to your schedule. It might be right after you wake up, or as soon as you crawl into bed in the evening. Don't worry about whether you're doing it right, or about all the thoughts that may swirl around. Just give yourself space, and know that success is you showing up and honoring this commitment to yourself. After you meditate, write out what came up. What were the thoughts, the ideas, the worries, or the visions?

CHAPTER 8

# Clearing the Path

Another way to describe a soul nudge is anything that your heart is truly craving: anything that you deeply want, under all the shoulds and other people's expectations. It's your higher self gently, lovingly giving you guidance, pointing you down the path that is meant for you.

Fear has come up so many times in this book already, and I want to talk a bit more about why. You might not even consciously know it, but fear is holding you back in so many ways. That's true for most people. Fear can stop you from taking action. It can mess with hearing your intuition. It can block soul nudges sometimes without you even knowing it. It's that moment when your brain blocks out a possibility, blocks out even a faint idea, because your ego says, "That's not meant for me." There might not even be a reason that comes into your brain for why it's not possible, or your brain might just move on to another thought, passing over what could be a vital piece of information.

All fear is real, but what you're afraid of might not be. Your body freaks out to keep you safe, and you get to tune in and understand what's actually right in front of you. It can be a true survival instinct to avoid a dark alley at night—or it could be your brain running wild, imagining all the terrible things that could happen. The fears "I might fail" or "I might run out of money" can represent real concerns, and also be worries your brain has exaggerated. You get to dig in and ask yourself what is true in the moment. Are you actually failing? Are you actually out of money and unable to pay rent and bills? Are you actually in a situation that feels dangerous?

Most fears seem real because they could come true, yet they aren't the reality in the moment. Calling this out helps calm your brain and your body. Take it one step at a time, and see if the same fears come up when you think only about the next step. If your dream is starting a business, the next step might be creating your offer and getting your first client. Taking that step doesn't mean you have to leave your job and a steady paycheck, which likely eliminates some of the money worry. Once you take the first step, you'll have income flowing in, and the money fear might not be right in front of you anymore. Digging in helps you see what steps are being asked of you, and if the fear is being inflated as you think about moving forward.

This process is so key as we wake your dream up. What does your soul need to open up and let you know where to go next?

## Chapter 8: Clearing the Path

It needs to feel safe. Your ideas need to feel safe. Your inner child needs to feel safe, loved, heard, and secure.

That sounds vague, unhelpful, and kind of like a lot of work, right? So here's where we'll start.

Write out things you'd do if you weren't scared. What would you take on? What would you try? What ideas and cravings need to be seen and heard? Even if those ideas might seem silly or impractical or even irrelevant, notice what comes through. What energy do you feel thinking about them? Maybe you feel warrior energy when you think of that tattoo you've been wanting. Maybe you feel calm when you picture the yoga retreat you've wanted to attend, but have been scared to do alone. It's important to not only see the ideas, but what you'd feel when you say yes. Those feelings show you what your heart, soul, and body are wanting.

I also want you to write down the people you feel jealous of. Write down the things you see other people doing, the things that make you think, "That's super cool." Write down the name of any person about whose life you've thought, "I wish I had that."

Specifically, write down what stands out. It could be about the person, or about their life. It could be that the person is someone who speaks their thoughts without holding back, without a single concern about what people think. It could be that the person wrote a book and is traveling the world. Whatever you admire or feel jealous of.

Jealousy is so often thought of as a negative emotion that we should suppress or ignore. But it can be a powerful tool to show you what you want, yet don't believe is possible for you. The same is true of judgment. We can be jealous of and judge the things we crave but haven't allowed ourselves to experience.

Instead of fighting it and feeling bad when those feelings come up, invite them in. Every emotion is trying to tell you something. The sadness shows where pain has been stored up. The happiness shows what your heart enjoys. The jealousy shows what you're truly craving.

Take a look at the list of people you're jealous of. Notice any themes that come up. Do they do a similar type of work? Have a similar lifestyle? Embody certain characteristics?

What can you see that you want from this list? What type of person do you want to be? What might you want your work to include? Write these out, and pick one or two that feel the most exciting to do, have, or create.

With that list, notice what thoughts come up. What are the reasons you haven't let these areas of excitement turn into goals? Why have you seen other people doing these things but haven't tried for yourself? If you picture writing the book, taking the trip, or owning the business, what are the first thoughts in your head? Write those down.

I'll bet you'll notice those thoughts are actually bullying you.

"You don't have time."

"You haven't saved enough money."

"You don't have enough clarity yet."

"You have no idea how to do that."

Keep writing out those thoughts, whichever ones you've heard in your own mind. All these thoughts and worries are constantly running around in the back of your head, whether you realize it or not. That voice is scribbling on your ideas, on your soul nudges, on your intuition, until it's hard to see it or hear it.

Your idea, your dream, your purpose is like a seed. It's a little fragile. It's ready to grow, but it needs the right environment. Your number one job is to create that.

Start loving yourself, and trusting that you're here to do big things.

Reduce the mean girl thoughts, and replace them with more support, love, laughter, and fun.

Realize how powerful you are and what your talents are.

Release the stories of not deserving it or not being worth it.

Let in guidance, support, love, and trust.

Keep writing out those mean thoughts and worries, the way your brain beats up on you. Write them on one piece of paper, and feel free to color, to draw, to put whatever you need to on the page that gets the energy out of your head, and onto paper.

Then, on a new piece of paper, write out what's actually true. Things like, "I can figure it out," or, "The support and guidance I need is right in front of me."

Write whatever feels true. Whatever you actually believe. Do this as many times as you need until your head feels clear. You're inviting in new thoughts and beliefs, and clearing space for the ideas to actually land.

*SOUL NUDGE: UNCOVERING WHAT YOU'RE MEANT TO CREATE*

CHAPTER 9

# Give Yourself Some Credit

Calling out the thoughts that are bullying you is a process you'll need to do time and time again. It's easy to skim the surface and just list one or two thoughts, or skip the activity altogether. It can be uncomfortable to feel how you've been talking to yourself and the emotions associated with that.

When I first listed all my thoughts, I was shocked by what the soundtrack of my mind sounded like. It took some time for me to clear out the gunk: the thoughts that I was too young to be an entrepreneur, that things would all fall apart, that going solo was too risky, that no one would like what I had to offer. I had to call out those thoughts like the bullies they were.

Sometimes those negative thoughts can be so persistent and so stifling that it's hard to even hear past them: to hear what we want. I ask the women I work with, "What do people say you're best at? List any skills/traits that come to mind. What do you feel most confident/excited doing?" Many of them struggle to answer. Some of them have to ask the people around them to get even the first few things on the list. That breaks my heart a little because I truly believe we all have gifts and ways we can help the world. Our loud, mean thoughts can beat us up and prevent us from feeling that truth.

When I asked this question of one of my clients, she had to really think about it. She told me, "well that's actually the issue… I feel like I don't have any skills." So I re-phrased it to her, asking what she has the most fun doing. She told me that she loved listening to other people, that she was the go-to for all her friends when they had problems, that she was a great problem-solver, and that she loved writing. Of course, all those things are skills. She, like many of us, thought she needed to be the best at something in order to own it as one of her skills.

There are innate parts of who you are that also contribute to the talents you have. Curiosity. I was always the kid asking who was on the phone whenever my parents got a call, not because I was snooping and wanted to do anything with the information, but just because I was curious. I wanted to know things. I'd always ask questions about what happened in people's days just because I wanted the information. That curiosity is a trait and a skill, and now plays a huge role in how I coach my clients and get to the bottom of what they're feeling and what they need next.

Notice the noise and the mean thoughts. But also list your talents, skills, and the things you're good at or love to

CHAPTER 9: GIVE YOURSELF SOME CREDIT

do. This is the list of truths. Really feel this, and own it. You deserve so much more credit than you give yourself.

*One day I think you realize you'll never know if you did it "right."*

*No one gives you a grade,*

*Or a medal,*

*Or a certificate of completion.*

*You just keep moving forward.*

*Sometimes feeling more lost than others.*

*And, in the end,*

*You're the only one who knows how it all played out.*

CHAPTER 10

# Growing Pains

What I absolutely want to normalize with this process are the growing pains that can happen on this journey. I think sometimes when I talk about " soul nudges," people take that to mean that once they say yes to those nudges, it's smooth sailing from there. The whole picture? soul nudges bring you opportunities to grow and step into a new version of you. That doesn't always feel easy.

I felt that clearly when I decided to move, and started looking for a place for us to live in San Francisco.

In crisis communications, I had to manage and make room for several different potential outcomes of any given situation, so I thought I was prepared. I had my folder with every resource, credit score, and reference I thought I could need. Some places even asked for pictures of our cats—and I seriously had the cutest ones.

As I marched up to the first open house, I saw a line. For the coffee shop next store, right…?

Turns out, the huge line out the door was for the open house. It looked worse than a Black Friday sale. Everyone was pushing. The woman showing the place wouldn't speak more than two words. Apparently it was a race to the finish line because everyone was scribbling madly on the application forms. I then came to learn it was first come, first served. Literally the first person to hand in that form would likely get the apartment.

I had no chance. My husband was still up in Seattle, not even there to fill out a form. I was so overwhelmed. I left the apartment, went out onto the street, and lost it. Hysterically crying. Calling my husband to say we couldn't actually move anymore. I felt lost. Alone. Exhausted.

Our method of apartment hunting had been me flying down first thing in the morning on the 6 a.m. flight and coming home by 9 p.m. on the evening flight. That first day was shot. I hadn't planned for this.

I started getting better at it, or at least better prepared. But let's just say that trying to find a place that didn't have a major flaw was a true lesson in dedication. This book isn't about apartments in San Francisco, so I won't go into it…but yikes.

I was down to two days before I had to start my new job. And I had nowhere to stay.

There were some dramatic moments. Running all over town to five different open houses across the city. Not realizing that there were three different types of pub-

CHAPTER 10: GROWING PAINS

lic transportation: buses, a subway, and an underground train. Yeah, I waited at least 30 minutes at a bus stop when really I needed to be on an underground train.

Finally, the day before I had to start my job, I got a new apartment. It was the end of a long day, and I almost skipped the open house because I'd been to so many already, and this one was across town. Yet, something kept me going. I made it to the apartment, walked inside, and couldn't help but smile. I'd seen some pretty awful places, with tar smeared on the carpet or closets with wires hanging out. This one had beautiful wood floors, lots of sun pouring in, and trees outside the window. The man showing the apartment looked at my face and said, "You've been apartment hunting for a while, huh? I can always tell the ones who have by the look of relief on their face when they see something in this building."

I still had to trek across town, walking through some incredibly sketchy parts of the city, to turn in my application. Yet it all came together. I set my one suitcase down in the walk-in closet. Done. Mine. Accomplished. Somehow I manifested this one right under the wire.

The rest was supposed to be taken care of. One-day shipping on the furniture I needed. My husband driving down in a couple of weeks with the rest of our stuff to officially move into our new place. Easy.

Right?

Until 7 p.m. on my first night in the apartment, when the furniture company called. Our stuff hadn't made it onto the truck. Not happening. No other options. It wasn't going to arrive for another 24 hours. So I was in a new city.

No car. Didn't know a soul. And didn't even have a blanket or a pillow to sleep with. Not quite how I imagined it.

I asked our landlord where the nearest store was, and, luckily, got some decent directions. But I felt broken. This was too hard. I had obviously chosen wrong. I stood at the bus stop, bawling, and called my mom to say it was all a mistake. Whoever said taking risks was fun…that person wasn't my friend anymore.

I bought a pillow, a fuzzy blanket, and an air mattress. Rode a bus that terrified me. Didn't get too lost, or attacked by a stranger (true fears in my head at the time). I made it home, had pizza delivered, and ate alone in an empty apartment. But at least I had done it. I had survived. I had made it happen.

A few weeks later, my husband moved down with the rest of our stuff, and it felt like the puzzle pieces started fitting together. My nerves calmed down, and my excitement came back. The moments to get to that place hadn't been easy. I had questioned my decision to move about a thousand times. I'd wanted to turn back. I didn't understand why I'd had such a strong urge to move in the first place. I could have easily questioned if moving was truly a soul nudge, or if I had read my intuition wrong.

I share this story because the challenges don't mean you've made the wrong choice. You didn't hear the guidance wrong or mess it up. You actually said yes to exactly the right thing, and sometimes that comes with discomfort. It almost always means you're doing new things, shedding old stories, and stepping into a new version of yourself. The Universe is conspiring to turn you into exactly the person you need to be for your soul's mission, for your next steps.

I see this time and time again with my clients. For example, one client decided to take her business idea seriously. She paid for one of my programs, and we were just starting to dive in when her long-term relationship with her boyfriend ended. The thought came into her head that maybe now was the wrong time to start a business. Maybe her relationship ending was a sign that she wasn't meant to move forward with her ideas, and instead should focus on taking care of herself. Her brain so quickly wanted to reprimand her, to tell her she had "messed up" by taking the risk to start a business.

What actually unfolded was that the rawness she experienced in the breakup allowed her to discover her authentic self even more fully. The lessons she learned as she healed quickly turned into course content she felt passionate about teaching. She wouldn't be able to serve the clients she has today without the tools she gained during that time. Her business blossomed quickly once she embraced the thought that everything was actually perfect and stopped questioning where her intuition had taken her.

In this moment, I want you to write out what next step you could welcome in if you knew it was all unfolding perfectly. What would come next if you stopped worrying about whether you're making the "right choice," and surrendered to the fact that your intuition is taking you exactly where you're meant to go?

CHAPTER 11

# Where Can You Start?

One of my favorite things about soul nudges is that following one pretty much always opens the door to another. Moving was the step I knew at first. Once I acted on that, so much more opened up. At the time, I thought I just needed a change in scenery, when it turned out that moving was setting the stage for answers to so many of my deeper questions.

As my husband and I were getting settled in San Francisco, I felt like I was on a mission to do things differently: to make new choices to help me become the person I'd always wanted to be.

That involved a lot of changes. Eating better. Working out. Going to yoga. Making new friends.

Throughout the process, I also realized I wanted to start putting time and energy into my passion for writing.

I'd always loved to write. After moving to San Francisco, I felt inspired to write about what I was doing to change my life. At the time, that meant taking care of myself. Reducing my anxiety. Living in a way that felt good to me.

It only made sense to put it in a blog.

So I poured my heart out, writing about my feelings, the personal development work I was doing, the workouts I tried, and how I was moving through my anxiety and finding true happiness. It felt good to have a place where I was authentically expressing myself. Not being who anyone else wanted me to be, just sharing what was truly most meaningful. When I first started my blog, my mission was to prove life can be beautiful, satisfying, passionate, and inspiring—even when there are difficulties. I wanted to share stories, thoughts, inspirations, and tips that might motivate at least a few people. I was spreading the message that the only true form of success is true happiness.

There was one flaw in my plan.

I was nervous to be the face behind these thoughts. I didn't feel qualified to be giving advice. I felt that if my friends and family knew what I was writing about, I'd be labeled the weird one. I might get too many questions that I didn't feel ready to answer. So the blog wasn't in my name…and you probably couldn't have hunted me down as the author if you'd tried.

For a while, it was fun to simply write and let the messages flow through me. Eventually, though, the nudge came to actually promote my blog. To put it out in the world in a bigger way than a small Instagram handle and a WordPress site very few people visited. It was time to actually own that it was mine, and share it under my name.

## Chapter 11: Where Can You Start?

I remember the day I shared the blog on my personal Facebook page. I thought I would die.

What would people think? I was never the outspoken girl. I wasn't the one giving advice. I was the one quietly observing. This would probably make me seem weird. But I had to get it out there. I had to own the personal development conferences I was going to. The podcasts I listened to. The books I was reading. And I just had to see if it would help someone.

So I pressed enter. Closed my eyes, made it happen, and rushed in to work. Waiting for me on my desk was one of the sweetest Post-it notes I've ever seen. The words thank you, with a big smiley face, telling me, "Thank you for sharing." Throughout the day, I opened Facebook to messages filled with support and love. Over the next few weeks, I had conversations over coffee where I actually got to share what was in my heart in a much deeper way than I usually did with the people around me. It was terrifying. It was freeing.

I never want to forget that version of me—that girl who was bold enough to try: the one who spent her evenings and weekends, after 50- or 60-hour work weeks, writing blog posts, knowing that only five or ten people might read it. But that didn't matter. If the light helped one person, it was enough.

In that moment, I had tapped into something more powerful than I first realized. I had tapped into the power of knowing who my work could impact. I could picture the girl who had been dealing with anxiety, trying so hard to blend in at school or at work. I could picture her nerves about speaking in a group, her overthinking mind racing at all times. I knew how she typically did what she was told because it was easier, and protected her from standing out. Standing out only brought on more anxiety. So she became incredibly good at doing what was expected, at pleasing other people. Now, all of a sudden, she was realizing she had to learn how to be happy.

This was the person I was writing to. I didn't know all the ways I could help her, or what that mission would evolve into, but I did know who I was doing it for, and that in that moment I was starting with a blog post. I was doing something.

Your first Facebook post, blog post, or Instagram photo where you share your heart may only get a couple of likes. It's a normal part of the process of stepping into this new role. It can be terrifying to wonder what your friends are thinking, and why only a few people interacted when you spent so much time thinking about what to say. Your mind can start racing, worrying that it's embarrassing to have only a small number of likes, or to ask a question and have zero people comment with an answer. What gets you through it? Knowing everyone starts somewhere. I had my first post sharing my heart and soul, and it only had a few likes. In those moments you decide to keep going, to keep sharing, while picturing the person you're actually writing to. The person you're writing to, who needs your message and your light, the one that post is meant for. Picturing that one person who makes it all worth it, and gives you courage. Even if that person didn't find your first post, or even your second, think about why it's worth trying to reach her. Why does she need you, now more than ever?

Start to picture the person you feel most connected to helping. Who is the person you truly want to speak to, to reach, to impact in some way? You don't need to know how yet. Just write out as much as you can about who he or she is. What she's feeling. What his/her pain is. What challenges he/she is facing. Don't forget to include why you care so much about this person.

Write this out. Don't think too hard about it, just see what flows. Who do you want to touch with your work? Who do you feel connected to, maybe because you see a past version of yourself in her story?

If the answers flow, have a moment of gratitude for all the ways your soul is talking to you already. If you feel stuck in any way, keep reading. Write what you do know, and trust that more answers are coming as you keep moving forward.

*No one knows what's going to matter.*

*What post goes viral.*

*What poem becomes famous.*

*What quote becomes a catchphrase.*

*For every sparkle of success there are hundreds on the floor.*

*Attempts that went unnoticed.*

*The moments of courage that propelled the rocket into the air.*

*The dust that fell from the star.*
*Those are just as important.*
*They are pieces of your heart.*
*Be willing to let the first step be as significant as the step surrounded by applause.*

CHAPTER 12

# Overwhelmed by All the Choices?

Now you have a list of what you do know. You're starting to see what your ideal day looks like. You're making space to listen to the soul nudges that come through. And you even have a picture of the person you want to start helping. That's huge.

As you look at these lists, and even as you were creating them, a part of you might be struggling with what to pick. And once you start opening up your brain to the possibilities, all of a sudden a new problem or problems might rush in. What to pick? What's the right choice? What's meant for now?

I want you to take a second and think about what you value most in this moment. Not what you "should" value. Sometimes there's a pressure to answer family or friends first because of our connections with others. So set aside any guilt, and answer from your heart. What, at your core, do you truly value?

Is it travel? Freedom? Purpose? Fulfillment? Adventure? Peace? What value is bubbling up? Now notice if your actions honestly prioritize that value.

When I was in my corporate job, I would have absolutely said that one of my values was adventure, mostly meaning traveling. Yet, at that point, my energy and money were going other places. I wasn't actually prioritizing what I said I wanted, which left me feeling discontent and unsure why I was unhappy.

As you explore what's true for you, the Universe will likely give you chances to choose. You'll get to see if you're listening to your values, to the soul nudges, and what the Universe is trying to tell you, or if you opt for the more comfortable, safe choice.

Often, after my clients get clear on the person they're meant to serve, what their business looks like, and start helping their soulmate clients, they get presented with a choice. All of a sudden, they're given a promotion at work, but it means more hours on the job and less time to work on their business. Now, they have to choose. Do they trust the soul nudges they've received, the ones leading them to create a business and start on a new path, or take the comfortable promotion that seems like more of a guarantee?

I faced a big fork in the road after getting settled in San Francisco. Since starting my new job, things were better. At first, it felt like exactly where I was meant to be. The job was closer to what I wanted to do, and my blog and

## Chapter 12: Overwhelmed by All the Choices?

my personal development work were truly fulfilling. It all worked…for a little while.

Then, the company I was working for started going under. We went from around 85 employees to about 16 within eight months. Most of the people who left did so voluntarily because our clients were leaving, and the company's leadership kept changing. Then there were few rounds of layoffs. I found out that we lost our biggest client while I was in Hawaii on my honeymoon.

Long story short: corporate life didn't feel so stable anymore.

I tried to make the best of my situation. Many people reminded me to be grateful of the income and the fact that I wasn't one of the ones let go, and so I did my best to stay positive. I spent my commute to work in the morning listening to inspiring podcasts, playing meditations, and blasting my favorite music. I felt great—until the second I walked in the doors of my office building. Then, it was like a cloud of heavy energy descending onto me.

I knew I had to figure something out, but I really didn't know what I wanted. I thought I had years to figure that out! Yet, all of a sudden, a real decision was in front of me. How did I want to make my income, knowing this job wasn't working?

Of course, my first instinct was to look at other corporate jobs.

Every time I did a job search I was discouraged by my options. I'd search many different keywords to see what sounded fun. Some openings were actually in the PR and marketing world, and others were for nannying or nonprofit work. I was searching for anything that might spark that thought of, "This is my next step." I would pull up job listings and feel physically ill. None of it felt right.

It was hard to explain. When I tried to talk about what I was going through, I could tell that some people thought that I was being snobby, needed to face reality, and would have to settle for something.

But I kept listening to the soul nudges. I knew how deeply I craved a feeling of fulfillment, and a life that felt like I was making an impact. So many of the jobs I was looking at didn't fit that description. They might have felt stable or comfortable or closer to what I knew, but they weren't meeting that deep hunger in my heart.

So I kept exploring, keeping fulfillment top of mind. I started helping non-profits to see what they needed that I was able to do. I set up tons of coffee chats with people I thought were doing cool things. I started exploring everything that was out there—the crazier the better. My soul was telling me to look at what was possible.

In the meantime, though, my brain was kind of freaking out because what I was doing didn't fix the immediate problem of needing a job, needing money, and desperately wanting to have a plan and know the next couple of steps. The one thing I could say is at least I was doing something. I tried to keep an open mind and an open heart, and view the process as exploring what lit my heart up.

The Universe certainly delivered all kinds of opportunities: writing blog posts for non-profits, bringing water to rural cities, and helping children learn self-love. Event planning with energy healers (with the added bonus of energy healing and chakra clearing for myself). Talking to people who had written books, were traveling the world, were coaching or holding retreats, and who healed others with practices I'd never even heard of.

Talking to people doing these things lit my fire even more.

There were all these amazing people, engaged in incredible work. Sharing their gifts. Living a life so different from what I'd ever seen. Some were just starting. Others had been on this path for years. To me, it didn't matter. I was in awe of each of them, and of the courage it took to dream an idea and actually make it happen.

Take a moment to write this out for yourself: In this moment, who are you feeling called to talk to? What spaces have been interesting you? What topics have you loved learning about, and who are the leaders in that area? If you were to set up coffee with someone who inspires you, who would that be?

*What if you didn't have another year*
*to make that dream happen?*
*Not another year,*
*Another week,*
*Another day,*
*What if it came down to today?*
*What would you do differently? And*
*what rules would you break?*

*Because sometimes you have to make
a mess to move forward.*

*You can't be afraid of breaking a few
things while you're running.*

*But then there's that freedom,*

*The wind in your hair. Your arms flying free.*

*And that's when you know—you
wouldn't have it any other way.*

CHAPTER 13

# Owning the Path You're Meant to Take

There's another piece of the puzzle that makes up this path, one that your brain can't help you find. As you open yourself to your soul nudges, it's also essential that you open yourself to trust in the Universe.

Since you picked up this book and you've read this far, I'm confident that you're defining spirituality in your own way. You might have your own practices and rituals, or be exploring what feels right to you. New books, new ways of healing, and new ways of connecting with the Universe are likely coming into view. Sometimes that brings up fear, especially fear of judgment from those around you.

Religion was a complex topic throughout my childhood. My dad used to be a minister, and my mom was raised Catholic. My mom loved learning about religions from a cultural perspective, and even taught at a Jewish school. I was raised in a Lutheran church, and went to Sunday school most weeks of my childhood.

I didn't realize it at the time, but when I was younger I was already very intuitive. I saw signs from the Universe all the time, especially 11:11 (which is considered a sign of a spiritual path), and made it a practice to set intentions for the day when I saw these symbols. I was extremely emotionally sensitive, deeply intuitive, and extremely self-aware. On one family trip, I loudly declared that my goldfish, who was back at home, was dead. My mom looked confused, explaining that he had plenty of food, and we hadn't been gone long, and so of course he would be fine. We got home and, sure enough, my fish was dead.

Despite my intuitive, spiritually-inclined nature, I never felt quite at home in organized religion. When I was a teenager and it was time to be confirmed in the Lutheran faith, I made a strong case to my parents, asking not to take that step. It didn't feel right, I didn't feel fully devoted, and I didn't want to make false promises. My mom honored my emotional argument, and during that phase I really distanced myself from anything I thought of as religion.

Religion brought up a lot of debate and even outright argument between members of my extended family, who held different beliefs. So as I explored my own spirituality, I kept quiet, and later realized it was fear of judgment and controversy that made me keep my mouth shut. I was pretty sure that talking about my beliefs would mean lots of questions, criticism, and defending my opinions.

Even though I felt timid about exploring the spiritual

## Chapter 13: Owning the Path You're Meant to Take

side of things, I also felt drawn to it. When, as an adult, I started to talk to people doing cool things and volunteering with non-profits, I came across an amazing Australian woman who was starting out as a practitioner in a modality called "The Spiral." I'd never heard of it. All I knew was that there were levels of healing that went through each chakra and helped clear your energy. She was looking for someone to help plan and promote her workshops, and was interested in hiring me for that role.

Going into the conversation, I was very nervous. I had no idea what this type of healing really looked like, if it worked, or how it worked. Deep down, I wasn't even sure if I believed in this healing modality, not to mention whether I could help plan and promote an event around it.

We had a conversation about what her work looked like, how she got into it, and why she felt so passionate about it. After the first call, something in my gut told me I needed to take on this project. My brain was still freaking out about what in the world this "healing" did, how it worked, how she was qualified…but my body was all in. So I agreed to help, and she offered to take me through The Spiral so I'd know what it was all about.

I can't stress enough that there's a big element of surrender in the process of following your soul nudges. Of hearing your brain say, "Seriously…that's crazy," but trusting what it's leading to. Up until this point, I had engaged in healing in much more commonly accepted ways. I had done some massage and bodywork, attended some personal development events, and started meditating so I could connect with my soul on a deeper level. But I had no experience in the realm of energy work, especially in this capacity.

What did I have to lose, right?

We had weekly calls during which she asked me all sorts of deep questions. We used healing tools I'd never heard of. There were moments when what she asked felt completely ridiculous, even a little bit crazy. Sometimes my brain was loud, wondering if The Spiral was working.

Yet, sometimes the things that came out of my mouth amazed me. I was sharing things I'd never talked about before. I was crying all of a sudden, or angry, or nostalgic. I couldn't deny that I felt different after each session.

Each week I started leaning deeper into trust. Trust of what was happening. Trust of what I felt. Trust that I didn't need to know why it worked—I could honor my intuition to know if it felt right or was helping.

By the end, I had opened up in more ways than I could count. The biggest way was that I learned to trust. I learned to try new, "weird" things, just because my gut wanted me to. I learned to turn down the volume of my judgmental voice, and honor what my inner voice was saying. In that moment, I had to release the fear of judgement and allow in my own intuition and self-trust.

The lesson of trusting your inner voice comes up time and time again as you try new things, expand, and face new challenges. Your soul is part of your spirituality. So is your belief in something greater. Your belief that you're here for a reason. Your openness to discovering what that's meant to look like. It's natural to worry about what people think if you talk about these things. I'm pretty

## Chapter 13: Owning the Path You're Meant to Take

sure every single person who has gone through major changes, major growth, and a spiritual deep dive has worried they'd be seen as crazy.

It helps to focus on the bigger picture, and so I want to remind you of the person you imagined, the one you care deeply about helping. Think about the parts of your vision that have come up. Those things, those synchronicities and gifts of yours, aren't accidental. You won't be too much or too crazy for the people you're meant to find. Visualize the person you most want to help and most want to talk to, any time this fear comes up. They need your voice, your bravery, and your courage in this moment.

Find something you can use to symbolize your trust that your path is unfolding. It might be a quote, an affirmation, a crystal, or a picture. What reminds you that you're being guided?

CHAPTER 14

# What Comes After Yes?

At some point, we have to own what our soul nudges are telling us and take action on them. There is only so far that journaling and meditation can take us before it's actually time for change to happen.

As I kept exploring my own soul nudges, it became clear that I wasn't looking for the traditional path anymore. All the people I ended up talking to were entrepreneurs, coaches, yoga teachers, and healers. Those were the people piquing my curiosity, the people I wanted to hear more from. It hadn't yet crossed my mind to try to be one of them, to lead and guide others in that way. At first I didn't really know what I wanted. I just kept following the nudges to talk to people in that world.

I did start to put myself out there in the world and offer to help more people—some professionally, as clients, and some as part of my volunteer work. I wrote blogs for non-profits. I did some social media marketing and copywriting for women I felt were doing interesting and meaningful things. I ran fundraising campaigns for organizations, expanding their reach and impact. If it was a cause that pulled at my heartstrings, I'd do whatever I could to help.

That led me to coffee in San Francisco one afternoon with a Swedish woman, Sanne, who had written a book about starting a soul-led business. She had held retreats around the world, and was coaching women who were trying to figure out what to do with their lives. As I explained my situation—essentially waiting to be laid off, riding such waves of emotions from my personal life, and feeling completely lost and confused about what to do—Sanne stopped me.

"Do you hear yourself?"

I stopped. "Hear what?"

"You're asking for bad things to happen. You're waiting to be laid off. That's what you're hoping for. Instead of asking for something good to happen, this is what you're telling the Universe. You have to do something about it."

She then told me the story of her friend, who kept joking that being on disability would at least be a way out of her soul-sucking job. And then it happened: a car accident. And, of course, that wasn't better.

It really stuck with me. I usually made it my mission to be the one "doing the thing." Yet, somehow, I had stalled out—probably because I found the next step completely terrifying.

After hearing about the type of work I did in the cor-

## Chapter 14: What Comes After Yes?

porate world, the things I'd been reading about, and the topics that excited me, she said something I had no idea I needed to hear.

That I needed to start my own business.

She asked what I felt most confident helping others with. What I knew how to do from my corporate job. She encouraged me to really think about what offer I could put out in the world, not six months from now but in the next couple of weeks.

We spent six hours discussing the skills I had and where I could start. Not some fancy, long-term vision. Literally just the first step, which was determining the type of person I could help in this exact moment, and writing out how I could help them. At the time, my skills were copywriting and event planning, along with some social media marketing and management.

I ran home, literally tingling from head to toe. I spent a couple of hours creating a mediocre website, and then I set out to find clients.

I need to pause at this moment in the story to truly explain how much I was acting on what felt right, versus what my brain thought. In that moment I was highly caffeinated, but also truly lit up by an idea in a way that no job listing had ever made me feel. It felt terrifying, yet so exciting I couldn't deny that something in me wanted to make it happen.

I want to be clear that my head had a million objections. Yet, by taking action anyway, I chose not to listen to them. I chose to keep moving the energy forward that same weekend because I knew if I sat on the idea, I'd never do it.

This is why I feel so passionate about inspired action. Notice the soul nudge, which usually comes in the first few seconds after you think of an idea or an option, and honor it. Extra space doesn't usually mean more clarity. It actually leads to resistance and confusion. It leads to voices in your head telling you that you don't have time, or that tons of businesses fail, or that you need a website designer and fancy pictures to launch that website.

Instead of getting stalled by all that, I just started. I started without thinking about what I'd need to do a month from then, six months from then, five years from then. I just honored the idea, and did what I could in that moment.

As I've been helping people start their own businesses, I've been struck by how many of them are insanely overqualified people who still think they aren't ready. It comes back to this "I'm not good enough" track playing in their heads. Many of us have been hearing a variation on this almost since birth, believing we need more education, more training, and more experience before taking the next step. It keeps us consuming and striving. It's important to interrupt this cycle and realize when you do have what you need: You have the information, the tools, the practices, and just need to listen to your own wisdom. You just need to get quiet and apply it.

Even when my brain didn't feel like I was enough (I had more to learn! I was too young! I wouldn't know what to say or do!), I started surrendering and trusting that my soul did know. It has always felt deeply true that my soul carries wisdom from many past lives, wisdom so much older than I am. My friends typically joke that my soul is about nine million years old. So even if it's impossible for your brain to believe you have the answers…what if we just admitted your soul does? Your soul has got this.

Write that out, and really feel it. "My soul is leading the way, and she absolutely knows what she's doing."

CHAPTER 15

# You Actually Are Ready

I honestly thought about putting the entire previous chapter in boldface or something, just to really stress the importance of realizing how qualified you already are is to the process. One of the things I tell almost every single one of my clients is that you don't need to be fully healed to start healing others. No one has everything figured out, so start with something you can help with. That something can change and expand as you grow.

One key thing I realized after seeing it time and time again in myself and in my clients is that there's a huge reason most people don't feel ready. It's something so simple, yet so important.

You've had a front row seat to all the good, the bad, and the ugly in your life. I don't just mean the external things that happened, I also mean the internal things. The thoughts, the anxiety, the mistakes, the failures, the embarrassment—basically, the mess. With each of these moments comes stories that you form about yourself. Being the shy one, the anxious one, the one better at helping than leading. These moments add up, and form how you think of yourself.

But here's the truth. I'm pretty certain the way you see yourself is actually a version of you from the past.

Maybe you still identify as the shy one. The nervous one. The outcast. You have all these identities that may be from middle school, from college, maybe your first job. You aren't fully seeing the version of you that's here today, and how different she actually is.

The version of me from the past was the anxious one. The one who wasn't a natural leader. I had thoughts like, "I don't like change," and, "I don't typically take risks." That one went back to my fifth grade report card, where I passed every assessment except "risk taking." I failed that one. The teacher wrote that she wished I would raise my hand more in class and speak up more often.

There were a few reasons why I didn't do this. Part of it was not wanting to get it wrong, but the other part was the thought, "Do other people really need to know what I think?" After all, surely everyone else was having the same thoughts and coming to the same conclusions, figuring it out just as quickly as I did.

I wasn't giving myself any credit.

Those moments added up until I thought of myself as the quiet one. The shy one. Good at planning and preparing, but not typically the center of attention or star of the show.

All of these moments played in my head when I

## Chapter 15: You Actually Are Ready

thought of being an entrepreneur. Was I really ready for the stress of having my own business? Was I really able to be confident on sales calls? Was I really able to make this happen? All these thoughts hinged on the idea of who I was in the past. The anxious girl in high school. The stressed-out girl in college. The emotional, overwhelmed corporate employee.

What I wasn't seeing was who I actually was, in that moment. The one willing to move to a new city. To start a new job. To share her heart on a blog. To talk vulnerably with friends about anxiety and stress. The one committed to improving her own life, with a heart passionate about using that information to help others. My brain hadn't fully acknowledged, loved, and appreciated the me that was actually right here.

I want you to do that right now. Write out at least 10 reasons you're incredibly proud of the version of you here today. Most of my clients get to about seven reasons and then swear they're out of ideas. I tell them to keep going. Even if your list included 50 reasons, I'd still say you could come up with more.

Make this a daily practice. Many people talk about the power of writing out the things they are grateful for every day as a practice. I believe in including at least three things about yourself on that list. You are on an incredible, powerful journey. Give yourself credit for showing up.

CHAPTER 16

# Your Path to Leadership

There's a practice that goes beautifully with self-gratitude, and it's one of my favorite activities to do with my clients. Early on in our work together, I ask them to list all the things they're proud they've accomplished. I don't necessarily mean accomplished as in, graduated from or received a certificate for. I mean things they've made it through. The challenging times. The times they showed up and took a risk. The times they've followed their dreams.

I'm confident you haven't thought about those times enough. Recognizing what you've been through is what's going to allow you to keep moving forward. Some of those things may be filled with pain that you could be pushing aside or hiding from, even just a little. They are, however, a huge source of your power.

When I was eight years old, my father was hit by a car while out for a morning run. He suffered a traumatic brain injury and was airlifted to a local trauma hospital. All we knew at home was that he always took me to school in the morning after his run. But that morning, he never came home.

I remember my mom and I searching up and down his running route. I remember passing ambulances on the side of the road, just a block down from our house. I remember my mom looking worried, while my innocent child brain had me say, "Just keep driving! I'm sure he's down the road a bit. That can't be him."

We drove down the rest of his running route and never saw him. As we drove back and pulled over at the scene of the accident, I remember being told by a police officer that there was a "John Doe" who'd been hit by a car. I remember my mom turning white. We rushed to the hospital, me still innocently assuming that Dad would show up any minute. My mom knew otherwise.

The rest of the memories come like photos in a scrapbook. Seeing my dad, bright yellow from the drugs they gave him, lying on a gurney. Sitting in the family waiting room and waiting for ages. The doctor telling us he was in a coma, and they had no idea if he'd wake up. I was terrified to go into his room. The thought that kept going through my head: "That isn't my dad."

Over time there were other snapshot memories. Weeks where Dad hadn't woken up, and Mom would spend almost every day at the hospital. My family and friends all being at the hospital, wanting to talk to me when I just wanted to be alone. Teachers at school pulling me aside, even right as I went up to kick the ball for kickball. So many questions: "Are you okay? What do you need?"

All I wanted was to be treated the same as I always had. For things to go back to normal. So I decided to act like everything was fine.

I vividly remember the moment that I decided feelings were a weakness. My dad was in the hospital, and my brother told me to "take care of my mom." I decided that meant handling my emotions. My gift to everyone else? I'd take care of myself.

I would journal as much as possible, take time to let it out. But it always felt like there was a five-minute limit, a tool my dad had actually taught my siblings and me so we would be able to move past the hard stuff and keep moving forward.

This meant I pushed through the emotions during so many tough moments. The fact that in the past my dad sometimes chose to mow the lawn instead of coming to my school plays (granted, I'm pretty sure I was the rock on the side of the set, or something like that). Since he could no longer come, I quit drama. Or changing schools after the accident. There was a science technology program at my old school that my mom wanted me in. I wanted nothing to do with it, until I wanted to run away from all the people who knew me as "the girl with the brain-injured dad."

For a while, it felt like this moment defined me. Since my dad was incredibly involved in the community, what happened to him was talked about in a lot of different circles. He volunteered to teach science weekly at my elementary school. He had been in local politics. He ran Kiwanis Club, and was a leader in so many other local charities. He was the guy with the dahlia garden, constantly donating flowers and fruit from his 70-plus varieties of fruit trees.

He was so kind-hearted. But there was also another side of him that the accident brought out. He was in a coma for three weeks, and in the hospital for three months. The doctors warned us he'd have a more "extreme personality," even after recovering and leaving the hospital. Whereas once he could handle 10 minutes in a mall before getting maxed out, now he couldn't go at all.

The issue with this? My dad already had some pretty strong personality characteristics. He was driven. Stubborn. Motivated. A leader. Argumentative. And when all that became more extreme, it became very challenging.

Even just writing this is hard. I've done so much to make peace with my dad, our relationship, and our journey. Part of me doesn't even want to be writing these words anywhere they'll survive, because I feel bad having any record of his trying times.

But then as I'm writing this right now, two orange butterflies fly by. My sign from him, since he passed away. So I'm taking that as my beautiful permission slip to continue.

My mom planted the seeds for so many of my core beliefs, and my relationship with my dad is ultimately where I got my interest in the human personality. His reactions become irrational. He'd be angry at me for not answering the phone when a minute before I was forbidden from touching it. I started to get curious about what would calm him down. How I could evade trouble. What loopholes were there? Why did he think this way?

## Chapter 16: Your Path to Leadership

My mom says I was always the only one who could calm him down. What worked was laying out clear boundaries. You can't speak to me like that. This is what I'm willing to do. It no longer gets to sound like that.

What I could have never anticipated is how tied to my business my dad's spirit would be.

Every once in a while you read words that touch you and inspire you in such a way that your own thoughts and experiences suddenly make sense. Author Cheryl Strayed has written about her mother's death. She shared, "The strange and painful truth is that I'm a better person because I lost my mom so young. When you say you experience my writing as sacred, what you are touching is the place within me that's my mother. Sugar [the column she wrote] is the temple I built in my obliterated place."

My spirituality, my business, my writing, this book… you're touching parts of my dad.

You're feeling his desire to always make an impact. His constant questioning of how he could be of value. His kind heart, which led to him serving as president of multiple nonprofits, running for local office, volunteering weekly at our local church, and continually donating food, flowers, and money to charity.

You're feeling his stubbornness and dedication. Those qualities are a huge part of why I have a business to talk about, and a book for you to read.

And you're feeling his desire for his story to be shared. This probably isn't the form he imagined. But in the last year before he passed way, he was writing. He wrote a very small book, but one that held his story, his messages, and even recipes that felt close to his heart. Something in him knew his message was meant to be out there, and I have a feeling this is part of it.

Now, when I'm able to look back and connect the dots, it makes some sense. He was an entrepreneur, and the first seeds of my excitement around having a business were sown when I got to see the life he lived. He loved his work. He would always ask me questions like, "Do people find you useful?" Or when I was busy, he would say, "At least they need you!" I love that I got that from him. He saw success as being needed. Sales numbers were proudly talked about at dinner. Nap time was a shared activity between us at 3 p.m. He could take me to school while most other parents left hours before for work. I wanted to build a lifestyle like that. The freedom in my life to be able to structure my days however I wanted. That freedom was calling me…but "someday." Five years from now, right?

I could write an entire book just about what I learned from this time period in my life. I often think of my mom as Superwoman for getting our family through this time, and for all the ways she supported me. For so long, I considered it just something that happened to me, something I had to deal with. Yet, as I started this journey of understanding who I really am and what I'm on Earth to do, it became clear to me that everything happens for a reason. I needed to take every single experience, every single challenge, and put that into the column of reasons why I'm absolutely qualified to help other people. So while what makes you ready might not be a certificate or a training, your life has been getting you ready all along.

Take a moment to write out some of the big moments in your life and what you learned from them. Write out the turning points in your life: The challenges, the successes, the moments that stand out in your mind. Think about what happened during those times, and also what the Universe showed you during and after. For each one, think about why that experience might have happened. Why does that moment, that lesson, make you exactly the person meant to help others? The Universe is molding you into the leader you're meant to be.

*Some days pain can be turned into power,*

*And other days it just hurts.*

*There's something so powerful about letting things be messy sometimes.*

*Days without showers,*

*Pillowcases damp with tears.*

*The messages left unopened.*

*This is a place we all visit sometimes.*

*Scared. Healing. Worrying.*

*A home we need, but don't always want.*

## SOUL NUDGE: UNCOVERING WHAT YOU'RE MEANT TO CREATE

CHAPTER 17

# What Happens After the Leap?

After taking the leap and launching my business, at least in its first iteration, I needed to find clients.

This can feel like such a messy time for many entrepreneurs, because not only are you learning so many new things in terms of marketing, PR, branding, and how to put yourself out there, but you're also clearing many disparate thoughts: Am I good enough? Is this going to work? Is this even possible?

That's why, with every one of my clients, I start by talking about what they're confident they can help with. For example, one client was nervous about saying she could help solve anyone's problem, and kept saying maybe she wasn't ready. We went through this process, and she realized that her fear was around creating a program to help people who went through trauma, but she did feel confident working with artists and creatives who wanted to bring more joy, fun, and freedom to their craft. She realized she didn't need to solve every problem for everyone, just a certain problem for the people she felt legitimately excited to work with.

The question, "What am I confident I can help others with" was my guiding light as I started my business, and, in many ways, it still is. What do I feel confident I can help with, and what will make the biggest impact? Those questions moved me through fear to exactly where I was meant to go. It led me to my first couple of clients, where I went from pure copywriting to helping women create new offers and programs that attracted their ideal clients. It led me to enough clients that I was able to replace about a quarter of my corporate income. It continued to guide me as I figured out how to take my business from part-time to full-time.

Those questions also guided me as I went into some very new territory. It led me back to that idea of being a coach. Within a couple of months of working with new clients and really asking myself what they needed most, suddenly a coaching offer was coming out of my mouth.

I started where I felt comfortable, first with copywriting, then with a strategy session to understand my clients' businesses and visions, and then with me writing webpages, social media content, and branding strategy. I felt passionate about making sure my clients got results, which I knew would mean more clients and more interested leads. As I kept that goal of getting my clients results in mind, I noticed that things in my program needed to shift. I could spend hours writing beautiful, powerful website copy that the client loved—and then notice they never posted it. Or I could dig in with a client about why they wanted to launch a new offer—and then find them giving me generic answers versus the passion I expected.

So instead of offering just one call to strategize before I began writing, I started offering two calls. And then three. And then four. All to get to the bottom of what clients truly felt called to offer, and to illuminate the fears holding them back from actually talking about it and putting their content out into the world.

I started to offer the meditations and journaling prompts I had been using, which helped them get clear on what their mission was and what they were meant to be doing. I began talking through the tactics I'd used to quiet my own anxiety and noise so I could show up and do the work my heart wanted to. All the tools I'd used on myself were suddenly relevant to share.

Then it hit me: I was coaching. There it was, that thing I wasn't "ready for." I had tiptoed my way into it.

When I first felt the tap to become a coach, I felt so unqualified that I literally ignored the calling. Less than two months later, as I let my intuition lead the way and get even louder, I was launching my first coaching program. I knew what type of person I could help. I knew how I could help them. To me, that felt a lot different than just deciding one day to call myself a coach.

My goal with starting my own business wasn't necessarily to be a millionaire, it was to have time to myself to meditate and journal in the morning, and to do work I loved that provided enough money to pay my bills.

As I took steps forward, I kept that goal in the front of my mind. I wanted to prove it was possible. Before I moved, I heard my boss say that it was actually impossible to be deeply lit up by your job, repeating the saying: "That's why they call it work."

I turned to him and said, "I'd like to challenge you on that. Give me five years. I'll prove you wrong."

In short, I was on a mission. And there's no motivation quite as powerful as a heart set on helping people, and a fire to prove that the life of your dreams is actually possible.

Right now, I want you to think about why you're doing this. What's the fire in your belly, in your heart, in your soul? Why do you care so deeply about this path, and moving forward on it? Write out the thoughts that fuel you.

CHAPTER 18
# Things Will Get in Your Way... Do It Anyway

There usually isn't a perfect time to make a change in your life. That's one of the reasons I ended up quitting that corporate job I'd moved to San Francisco for on a random Thursday.

I was exhausted from commuting all the way across the city to work 9-5, supporting my clients on evenings and weekends, taking care of myself, and spending time with my husband. I could make time for it all to happen, but my energy was getting drained quickly. There was a part of me that was scared to take on more clients, because I wasn't sure I had the energy to support them.

Along with that, the environment at my corporate job wasn't exactly inspiring. People were leaving every week as the company continued to lose clients. There was very little optimism filling those walls.

I was tired, and not just from trying to do too many things in one day. I was drained from doing things that weren't nourishing my soul.

So I quit. I had hit the point when I couldn't do it anymore. I didn't even realize how big of a leap of faith I was taking. I just knew I had to leave that job, and I'd figure it out.

I kept telling myself that, in order have to something that most people will never have, you have to do something most people would never do. I asked myself if it was worth a year of some sacrifices to create my vision. To truly serve. To be able to say, "I change lives." To create a life that lit me up. The answer was always yes. It just was.

And the best part? It wasn't a full year of sacrifices.

The decision to leave that corporate job led to an intense, amazing, insane, and powerful next couple of months. In hindsight, I'm actually glad I went in a little bit blind. Now that I work with women starting a business, I see how the story "It's going to be hard" or "I might fail" stops people from even getting started. I had practically the opposite story in mind. I was going to figure it out.

I was also reminded by my coach and close friends that the worst case scenario in leaving my corporate job was simply taking another full-time job, which is exactly where I started. So really, what did I have to lose?

Yet, even as I was constantly reminding myself of those things, the first few months started to test my confidence. I suddenly had all this time to work on my business, and honestly no idea what to do with it. I'd make some Facebook posts, set up a couple of networking calls…and then, an hour later, I'd have no idea what would actually increase the odds of making a sale beyond writing some affirmations and hoping something fell into my lap.

That felt scary. Since I quit on a random Thursday, I hadn't exactly saved a huge amount of money as a "just in case" fund. I had a short runway until I'd have to go find another corporate job to support myself while living in an expensive city like San Francisco.

On top of that, less than a year after moving to San Francisco and a month before my wedding, my dad passed away. It would've been such an easy reason to put everything on hold, and to do the safe thing and stay in my corporate job. It could've been a reason to stop dreaming about entrepreneurship. But instead, it became my biggest reason to keep going, to keep exploring the ideas that excited me. The raw pain I was feeling made me assess what really made me happy.

In the first blog post I made after he passed away, I wrote, "Dealing with large emotional events, positive or negative, really helps you reassess your routines and the things you let into your life. When your life is filled with goodness, or with sadness, it makes the mediocre or negative things really stand out. Only recently with the large life changes I've experienced, did I realize how much of a negative impact the word 'should' carries. Even when dealing with the grieving process, I only gave myself about a week until the word 'should' started popping up and controlling my actions. 'I should call this person. I should go to this social event. I should stick to that commitment.' When you're emotionally raw, it's even easier to see the impact doing a 'should' activity has on you. It weighs you down. It takes more energy than you expect."

There's almost always a good reason why now isn't the ideal time. Maybe you were thinking of starting a business, and then got a promotion at work. Maybe you were ready to leave your job, and then some unexpected bills came in. You "should" save up more money. You "should" do another training. You "should" just give it more time. Trust me when I say, it's all part of the journey. You're getting the chance to choose something different. To interrupt a pattern that may have re-played itself about a million times without you knowing it. Has money prevented you from following your dreams in the past? Did you take a job that didn't excite you because it felt safe and secure? Did you pass up on traveling because you didn't have time? That pattern, that reason for not doing the thing, might show up again soon. You get to choose differently so you can go somewhere different in your life.

I've seen something exciting happen with so many coaches, healers, yoga teachers, personal trainers, artists—really, everyone I've worked with. When you're feeling called to help others, to truly serve the world in some way, a huge part of your healing is actually doing the work and helping others. I don't honestly think you can sit and journal or meditate your way to feeling whole and fulfilled. Part of your healing comes from taking seriously that you have a gift to share, a message to share, and a purpose in this world that is meant to help others.

I'm positive you have a part to play. You have a gift that people need. And the world is hurting. So while the

## Chapter 18: Things Will Get in Your Way...Do It Anyway

thoughts in your head might be, "Am I good enough?" or, "What I do isn't enough," or, "She doesn't mean me...I don't do work like that," or even, "I'm not ready...," in this moment, you get to choose a different story.

It's critical that you take steps forward, and seeing what comes up. See the fears. See the frustrations. See the areas where you soar, and the other places that don't quite go according to plan.

You might not feel ready, yet you're craving the moment where the vision all comes together. You want a direct, quick path from where you are now to your dream.

The truth is that it will happen so much faster than you think once you start moving. Are you waiting for the whole path to show up in front of you? Are you asking for a map in your hand before you take a single step forward? If so, it's going to feel like a long way away.

A friend of mine once described the importance of sending a "ship" out every day in the name of your dream. A ship could be meeting a new networking contact for coffee. Hiring a coach. Starting a new workout routine to energize you. The reason to think of them as ships is because when a ship used to leave the harbor, it was usually in search of gold. The reality was, some came back with gold, some with exotic spices, and some were even destroyed. Some came back quickly, and others had a really long journey around the world.

Your ships will add up so much more quickly than you think. I've had many ships that I thought were lost at sea, but that came back, months later, with pure gold.

The other thing my friend recommended was writing

down all the ships you send out, and circling the ones that came back. This is a small step that makes a big difference.

Take a moment to write out your ships. What actions have you been taking, and what actions are coming up? Are you noticing and appreciating all your efforts? Don't forget to show yourself everything that you're doing right.

CHAPTER 19

# It's Meant to Feel Messy

After you acknowledge how different the version of you here today is from the past you, you also get to acknowledge that the growth you've experienced is why you're ready to help others. You've learned so much from each challenge you've overcome. You've readied yourself with each step you took to improve your life, improve your health, and improve your happiness.

As I started working with more and more clients, I realized my anxiety wasn't just something I was meant to overcome. It was actually a big part of how I would help the world.

At first, I thought my anxiety gave me all the reasons it didn't make sense to start a business. After all, there had been a time when I was having anxiety attacks most weeks. I was hospitalized twice for abdominal pain they could never diagnose. I was given anxiety medication but chose not to take it. At one point, it made me anxious to even go up and order food or make a phone call.

Other people might not have recognized that I was struggling. I spent a lot of time trying to hide it. I remember dreaming of being a journalist, but worrying I couldn't do it because it was a "high-stress job," and my anxiety was bad enough without adding any extra stress.

I even based my college choices off of it—with a GPA and extracurriculars that could have gotten me into most colleges, I shied away from even applying to Ivy League schools. I worried that the pressure cooker environment would be too much for me.

I did somehow end up in a crisis communications job, which I'm now confident the Universe orchestrated on purpose. I spent all this time avoiding the stressful situations, so I was placed in one that made so much bubble to the surface. I was coming home crying after work. I wasn't happy, and I didn't know why. My mind was constantly racing.

It may seem like an odd jump that just a few years later I decided to start my own business.

The truth? I spent a lot of the first few months as an entrepreneur quieting the anxious voice I'd let run in the back of my head for so long. I listened to the critic inside me ask worriedly, "What if this doesn't work?" "What if I'm not good enough?" "Why would someone want me to help them?" "What if I can't get them the results they want?" I could go on and on.

I knew I had to get that voice under control. I chose to call it out, to notice what was true versus what was that anx-

## Chapter 19: It's Meant to Feel Messy

ious voice beating me up. My coach called her "that little bitch" so I could see how much that voice was bullying me.

Every entrepreneur faces obstacles. One of the things I love best about working with entrepreneurs is going deep into what they need most to make their business thrive. In my case, at that time, I didn't need a marketing plan or a sales funnel. I needed to boost my confidence and get my thoughts under control.

My anxiety also showed up in the thought that I didn't want to be the "star." As a journalist, you tell other people's stories. In PR, you support other brands, companies, and causes. Even when I first started my own business, I was really focused on event planning and copywriting—both things where I was mostly behind the scenes, making other people look good.

I had convinced myself I didn't want to be the star, when the truth is that it was just a lot more comfortable not to be. I had worn labels like "anxious" and "shy" for so long that it felt like I couldn't want to be the center of attention. But as I started to shed those labels, I started to get the nudge deep in my belly. As I was working on virtual assistant work for other entrepreneurs who were truly shining, this little voice was saying, "I could do what they do," and, "I could help people in an even bigger way." Even though at first it was new and exciting to help people as an assistant, it quickly became a title I was hiding behind.

I can't stress enough that you don't have to have all of your healing "handled" before starting to help other people. I could have easily let the negative thoughts and overwhelm prevent me from moving forward. I had a lot of fear and anxiety bubble up after leaving my corporate job. A lot of those old stories that I thought I'd left in high school began popping up in my head again.

It even showed up in the story of "I'm fine" after first quitting my corporate job. I wanted to be fine doing it on my own. I wanted to be fine figuring it out. I wanted to be fine being independent, being strong, being capable. But "fine" was hiding all the fears, all the feelings, everything my body was telling me. "I'm fine" kept me from asking for help at times I really could have used it. While I appreciate the qualities of determination, grit, and perseverance, I also bottled up much that I could've moved through in the moment.

I bet you can think of your own examples. How many times have you pushed through fear? How many times have you done something you didn't want to because you "should"? How many times did you bottle up your feelings?

If you're like me, you could probably answer "a lot" to all of those questions.

Now, as I built my business, I was being asked to operate in a whole different way. Instead of just ignoring all the feelings, my new focus asked me to sit with them. To heal them—not in a way that prevented me from taking action and helping others, but in a way where my feelings held hands with my goals. My soul and her big, badass, amazing goals built a relationship with my body, which would get overwhelmed or scared or anxious about what the next step was.

There were days when my own insecurities would bubble up so intensely that I'd spend hours sitting on the floor crying, just to get up and take sales calls that afternoon. It felt like I was a ping pong ball, flying between healing and action.

Looking back, I wouldn't have it any other way.

Each moment of healing, each moment of pain that I took time to see, feel, and sit with, was matched by an equally significant moment of gratitude. Sometimes it was gratitude for the ability to go for a walk on a gorgeous, sunny day. Some days, it was gratitude for a midday nap. Almost every day, it was gratitude for the clients I was getting to work with. My business was evolving quickly, and within a couple of months of hearing the idea, "You should be a coach," I had moved from copywriting to business coaching. It was lighting my whole body up. Instead of just focusing on the words on the page, I got to talk about soul connection. About why my clients had started a business. About how to attract the people they were meant to serve.

I got to combine my marketing and PR world with my years of personal development work. Asking the question, "What would make the biggest impact?" led me to realize that the women I wanted to help needed not only marketing tools but also a support system while they grew. My journey, and being in powerful spaces with other women entrepreneurs, had shown me that so much growth and change happens when you say yes to this work, and the leader you're meant to be. The women I felt so passionate about helping needed support for each step of that, not just a business plan and a pretty website.

Getting on calls with them was what kept me going. That's another big reason, while maybe a selfish one, that it's so important to get started. I always say the first year of entrepreneurship is like a self-development bootcamp. What gets you through is actually seeing the impact you're making and knowing the names and stories of the people you're helping. It's more than just a social media following or a blog with some likes and comments. It's about having people in front of you, ones you know you're helping. My clients were so frequently my motivation. I wanted to learn the lessons, have the experiences, and grow as a person so I'd be able to help them through the same things.

Each moment of discomfort, each tear, each bout of doubt, was made so much better when I saw my clients gaining clients. Gaining confidence. Getting clear on their purpose. Connecting with their souls. Leaving jobs, cities, and life situations that weren't serving them. Understanding how to make money from their passions. It made it all worth it.

*The core of your true self is never lost.*
*Let go of all the pretending,*
*and all the becoming.*
*All that you've done just to belong.*
*Curl up with your rawness and come home.*
*You don't have to find yourself;*
*you just have to let yourself in.*

CHAPTER 20

# Let It Keep Growing

As you keep growing yourself, your ideas, and your business, you'll likely feel some discomfort that comes when you try something new. There are growing pains that come with making a new offer, holding your first workshop, speaking on stage, and saying your new price for the first time. Get comfortable with a little discomfort, knowing that it's just because you're doing something new. The biggest growth comes from understanding how to support yourself and nurture yourself through the uncomfortable moments, so you can ultimately get where you want to go.

I had a few big realizations along the journey that helped calm my mind and my body on this unpredictable journey of entrepreneurship. This first one is huge, and I want you to remember it any time you have nerves or anxiety come up around taking the next step. "Failure" isn't really as much of an option as your brain builds it up to be. The actual reality is you pick an idea, try it, and pivot if it's not working. You can always make a new offer, try a different strategy, put yourself out there in a new way, and keep moving forward. As long as you stay connected to your passion, your soul, and what you are most deeply excited to create, it's more of "try again in a different way" versus "failure."

As I continued to grow my business, I saw how true this was. My income kept growing, but I still battled with the fear that it could all be taken away, or that the next month wouldn't size up as well. I had to experience the slow months for my brain to truly understand that, in the end, it would all be okay. The slow months meant making a new plan for the next month. They meant launching a new offer or switching up my marketing. There's a long runway leading up to most of the worries running around in your mind, and you get to pivot long before you get there.

The other thing that came up for me, and comes up with almost every client I work with, is overcoming fear of judgment. What will friends, family, and even random social media followers think about this new version of you, and your new path?

This shows up for my clients in many different ways: nerves about admitting they love crystals and energy work, fear of telling family about their new business, or worries about seeming different to their friends who've only seen the side of them that's drinking wine at 5 p.m. on a Friday. I remind my clients that the path they're

## Chapter 20: Let It Keep Growing

embarking on is different. Since it's different, people are going to ask some questions. If judgments come up, you get to remind yourself why you feel so passionately about this path. Who is it that you want to help? What have you felt or experienced that makes you feel, deep down, that this is the right direction? What is your truth telling you, regardless of what the people around you say?

It's also so important to remember that so often you're worrying someone is judging you, when the reality is you don't know what they're actually thinking. Getting peppered with questions doesn't necessarily mean they're judging you, and it could be that your brain is freaking out and projecting all the fears you have onto them. If you're worried about whether or not your business is going to be financially successful, it's not uncommon for a friend to ask you how many new clients you have. If you've felt nerves talking about the spiritual books you've been reading, someone is probably going to ask you about them and if you've truly found the information helpful. The judgment you're worried about getting from others is likely the judgment you're already subconsciously putting on yourself.

One of the most powerful things you can do is listen to those judgments and fears, and see what they bring up for you. If it's worries about being financially stable, what strategies and budgets can you put in place that make you feel more confident? If it's nerves around talking about the spiritual work you've been doing, write out why you're proud of yourself for doing that work. Why is it so important to you, and why is it something you believe in? As soon as you're rooted in your own truths, those questions from others will roll off you. As my clients move through their own fears and gain confidence in who they are and what they're offering the world, it's even common for the uncomfortable questions to disappear altogether. The Universe is reflecting back the areas you get to heal in yourself.

Another big thing I noticed over time is how often the judgments and opinions of others can show you the stories those people have been telling themselves. For example, when I first started my business, I heard a lot of people saying, "You're so brave! I could never do that. I've heard it's so hard to find clients." At first, people bringing up finding new clients would upset me. Were they saying I wasn't successful? That I wasn't good enough? Did it look like things weren't going well?

After observing people's comments, and getting tired of my emotional reactions, I started turning the questions around. I'd ask about what they'd be doing if they did follow their dream, whatever that was. I started seeing that their fears for themselves were linked to what they said about me. Maybe they wanted to start their own business but told themselves for years that "it's hard to make money with a new business," so they'd question me about my financial success. It wasn't actually about me at all. It was them facing off with stories they've told themselves for years, stories that probably kept them from doing things they really wanted to.

It's incredibly powerful to notice how many moments, people, and things can feed your fear brain. That's why it's so necessary to feed your happiness and belief brain every single day. You provide the fuel by writing out your vision, your why, the reasons you're fired up, and the things you can do throughout the day that bring you joy. It's your job to keep filling your cup so you can move forward with your mission.

What's feeding your happiness brain? If you're not already journaling on that, make time to write out the reasons you're proud of what you've been doing and creating. Add three things you can commit to doing that will bring you extra joy in the day-to-day, as you keep moving forward with your creations.

CHAPTER 21:
# Your Time to Come Alive

I'm very confident that a whole chapter, and maybe even a whole book, could be dedicated to aliveness. Life is too short and too incredible to not fully experience and love it. Yet, at one time, when I considered the qualities of a truly wild and free soul, my next thought would be, "I'm not like that."

Getting to the point of being completely free requires overcoming a huge amount of fear. It can be the type of fear so deep in your soul that you convince yourself you don't want that freedom. That it's too much work…that you'd sacrifice too much. That you want a life of peace and quiet that feels comfortable.

But here's the thing. That doesn't feed your soul. It doesn't nourish your potential. It doesn't push you to achieve your dreams.

Growing up, I always felt like the shy girl. I was so worried about what people thought, and I was afraid to stand out. But my heart wanted to be the free gypsy soul—soaking up the sunshine, jumping in the water, unafraid to follow my heart.

Sometimes our brain gets in the way when we consider, "What would make me happy?" or, "What sounds fun?" We all have so many stories, beliefs, values, and other people's opinions in between us and the answers to those questions.

During my healing journey, I realized the word "fun" went numb for me years ago.

I can't be sure of the exact timing, but I'm fairly positive that it started with my dad's car accident when I was eight. I developed an understandable fear of losing the things and people I loved. I felt anxious, and a deep sense of responsibility to take care of the people around me. My anxiety became so severe that I couldn't make it through a sleepover, even though I used to be the girl so ready to run off with friends at any time. I experienced intense worry about whether my friends and family would make it home, even if they were only two minutes late. I sobbed with every goodbye, because who knew if it would be the last one.

Essentially, I grew up fast.

I remember doing activities on the weekends or in my spare time and thinking, "People say this is fun...I guess this is fun?" I wasn't actually feeling joy in my body. Even things that were objectively fun often felt flat to me, like I was just going through the motions.

Describing this time has often been hard for me, because it sounds incredibly depressing when I put words

## Chapter 21: Your Time to Come Alive

to it. It feels important to stress that I wasn't having bouts of deep depression in this time. There were moments that brought joy. I was feeling the range of emotions in many other ways, and things did make me happy. But there definitely was a numbness and sadness to many moments that I couldn't fully explain.

Years later, as I continued to work with different healers and modalities, from reiki to meditation to shamanic work, the concept of healing my inner child came up over and over. For a long time, I focused on the trauma of it—my dad's accident, the fear, etc. And then, after one healing session, the focus started to shift. The magical woman leading the session asked me what made me smile.

The first answer that came up was bubbles. So she had me buy bubbles that I could blow any time I felt frustration. Instead of worrying about achieving a state of massive joy or finding things that felt fun, I started with what made me smile.

And the Universe let it get even better from there.

I was gifted an amazing opportunity to go to Costa Rica for a week after a year of intense growth in myself, and in my business. I actually knew very little about this retreat other than that I met the woman running it and we had an instant soul connection, diving into a channeled conversation about dark energy and the Universe and layers of healing. So when I had the chance to go, it was a clear soul yes.

This was something of a last-minute opportunity; I said yes less than three weeks before the start date. As the day quickly got closer, I was asked questions like,

"What's your intention for going? What are you going to work on there?"

I knew we were doing yoga, meditations, surfing, and SUP, and that it was a magical location. So the answer that kept coming out of my mouth was, "Even if it's just for fun, that would be amazing."

It turns out, fun was the key. In Costa Rica, I had no expectations. I knew I had to disconnect from work. It was my first full week without calls in about two and a half years.

Each morning we woke up and had a chance to meditate, often on the beach. And for me, that was pretty much always followed by jumping in the ocean. There was yoga, surfing, watching baby turtles hatch, movement classes, sound healing, and magic around every turn. As the week went on, I found my hair constantly covered in salt water, my body only wearing a bikini, and sparkles all over every part of me. I was genuinely skipping from place to place. There was glitter waiting for us before most of the yoga sessions, and you better believe it was dangerous to ask me for glitter—it would truly be an anointment.

There were a couple of people at the retreat I knew prior to the trip, and I heard the comment, "I've known you for years, and I've never seen you more alive." And I felt it. My heart was singing. I was playing. It felt fun. It was like I'd unlocked a new part of my heart.

I had sat with the pain as I was healing, and I was willing to cry about it. To feel it. To move heavy energy through my body. But now the work was letting the light in. When we dig into the depths, we are able to fly that much higher.

## Chapter 21: Your Time to Come Alive

This was proof. This was unlocking my inner child. My wild woman. My mermaid side. My priestess. My unicorn goddess.

In case you need a reminder: You have a version of all those parts too. You're on a journey to go find them.

CHAPTER 22:
# The Universe Is Listening

A big reason why you don't need to be ready before you start is because, as I've seen time and time again, the Universe will keep showing up to help you become the leader you're meant to be. As you dive in and understand who your soul is meant to help, and what your mission in this world is meant to be, the Universe starts responding—sometimes in unexpected ways.

For me, an unexpected turn was linked to my hands. I had eczema off and on my whole life, since the moment I was born. My mom says she took me back to the doctor the day after I was born because I had a rash all over my body. They could never figure out why.

It hasn't been that severe since, but throughout my life I would definitely get patches. As a kid, it was in the crease of my arm. In college, it became my wrists. I remember working in a soap and bath product store where we demoed products all the time, and I felt incredibly self-self-conscious touching the customers. There were times when it was really hard. But the eczema would eventually settle back down after a few months, and then disappear.

So when I first saw some eczema on my hands at the beginning of 2018, I wasn't overly worried. I knew how to deal with it—until it kept growing. It got much worse—redder, more swollen, more painful. I started trying almost every kind of healing you can imagine. I was open to everything, from lotions and creams to reiki, acupuncture, and meditation.

Nothing was working. Looking back, there were a few signs that some deeper healing work was coming up. When my eczema started popping up in January and in February out of nowhere, I started to feel a lot of heaviness in my heart. It was incredibly frustrating. Nothing was wrong. Nothing had happened. I'd been in situations that justified feeling real, deep, traumatic pain. So to feel this heaviness, this sadness, slowly creeping in over my heart for what felt like no reason…I didn't want to accept it.

I call it my dark week now.

In the weeks prior, the Universe had started making space for every frustration and fear of mine to bubble up. I had full weeks with back-to-back sales calls with potential clients—all of whom rescheduled. Things were falling through. Feelings were bubbling up. Until one day, the tears started—and not the kind that feel like they're going to end in an hour.

I remember telling my coach that I didn't know why

I felt so lost. I just couldn't help it. She told me to disconnect for a week, which I resisted—hard.

I gave in to a couple of hours of feeling it. My brain desperately wanted to get it knocked out, and not so secretly hoped that a few hours would take care of all these feelings. Yet, after sitting with the emotions for a bit, the words came tumbling out of my mouth. "I'm afraid to go into this darkness. I'm afraid I won't come back."

This wasn't a new feeling for me. When I was a child, I would lie in bed thinking about life and tuning into the energies around me. I can vividly remember that every once in a while it would feel like a dark storm cloud had formed overhead. I was terrified. I knew that heaviness felt like more than I could handle, so I blocked it out. Distracted myself. Pushed it aside.

But now I was in a totally different place. I was letting my gifts back in: being a deep empath, tuning into the energies of the souls around me, journeying. The heaviness wasn't going to let me push it aside. I had to dive into it in order to get where I was going. It was incredibly challenging to accept that I felt this heaviness without any particular reason. Nothing dramatic was happening in my life, in that moment. I just felt so many feelings, so much sadness.

Then started the week of darkness.

My coach told me to completely disconnect and really feel my feelings. That meant no journaling, because that led to trying to figure out the feelings, to explain them, and to fix them. No TV, no phone, no distractions. Nothing to numb out, and nothing to analyze the situation.

I was on a loop: crying, sleeping, and meditating. After the first day, I felt strongly pulled to read Louise Hay's book, *You Can Heal Your Life*. It didn't feel like an accident that this got added to the loop.

What came up was self-worth. Self-acceptance. Self-love. Pain and distrust of the Universe because of what happened to my dad. Pain from my dad. Pain from my inner child, who felt hurt and pushed aside more than I had realized.

It took three full days on that loop, knowing that nothing was fine, but it was going to be. When I came out, I'd never felt more reborn. The pain didn't vanish in a moment. But every part of me felt different. I still had some heaviness to shake.

I wanted to go to Sedona with a friend, but the trip wasn't coming together. We were both deep enough on the spiritual path to take this as a sign. We knew we could force it to happen, but it actually didn't feel like the right time. I felt frustrated. I still had some healing to do, and I wanted Sedona to be my magic cure.

Then, as I asked the Universe to give me what I needed to heal, to move forward, I received a Facebook event invitation from a woman local to San Francisco.

Not a coincidence.

She did shamanic healing. The event invite was for a couple of weeks later, when I'd be out of town at an event in LA. So I messaged her and asked if somehow, by chance, she could do a session the next day.

I bet you can guess what happened. I had the most beautiful healing session I've ever experienced. She

## Chapter 22: The Universe is Listening

tuned into the energy of what I needed, and said it was one of the sweetest messages she'd ever been called to pass along. All about receiving, and letting love in. Feeling your own love. Feeling your own heart. And letting in the life force of the Universe.

You are provided for. You are taken care of.

Cleansing in rose water. Leaning on the Universe. Clearing the heart.

And of course, feeling my dad's energy. Down to receiving the message to eat oatmeal, which he had done every single morning for as long as I could remember.

The most interesting part? The woman doing all this healing work on me had experienced severe eczema on her hands in the previous few years. This was a beautiful reminder that these messages are never sent by accident. Our souls truly are drawn to our teachers and our healers.

The session didn't clear my hands up, but it did open up a dialogue around what my hands were trying to tell me. I'll explain more in the next chapter about this, because it truly was a huge shift in my healing. It moved the physical symptoms from just frustrating and painful to an inquiry around what my body might be telling me. That shift was massive. Now, it's something I talk about all the time with clients.

Where can you give yourself gentleness, give yourself grace, for what you're going through? It's all here so you can heal it in yourself, and then heal it in others. So how can you let in some love for yourself and the person you're becoming?

Write out some areas where you are judging yourself. They might be points where you think you aren't "far enough along," things you've wanted to fix, or circumstances where you've been hard on yourself for how you reacted or how you handled the situation. Write out what happened, and also what you learned from it. Give yourself love for showing up for the moment, the challenge, and the lesson.

CHAPTER 23

# Keep Expanding Your Toolkit

My eczema wasn't going away, and now it's clear that was because it had more to show me and teach me. Keep this in mind with anything challenging going on in your life in this moment. It's here for a reason, and there might be many layers to that reason.

A few weeks after my healing session, the same woman who had led the ceremony announced she was leading a seven-month class that would lead to a 120-hour certification in shamanism, herbalism, and somatic coaching. The first time she mentioned it, my heart felt incredibly interested, and my head was insanely confused.

Diving even deeper into shamanic healing was a tap I never expected to get. I thought I was the girl who helped people start businesses. It got a little woo-woo as I incorporated meditation, yoga, and meeting your soul. But ceremonies, journeying, and herbalism were a whole new level.

Yet, those soul nudges kept coming. I knew I couldn't keep teaching other people to trust the nudge if I wasn't willing to keep trusting it myself. So the words, "Apparently I want to learn about plants," came out of my mouth.

That led to seven months of deep work in which I not only learned about plants but also dove deep into meditations, journeys, and ceremonies that had me exploring my past, my emotions, and my thoughts in a way I had never done before.

Part of why my brain justified saying yes was to see if anything could help with my hands. I was getting more and more worried as the rash started taking over my palms, my wrist, and each fingertip. The knuckles were the worst—they would crack and bleed. At times, it wasn't even possible for me to hold a teacup.

It was painful. It brought up a lot, especially frustration and self-blame. "What am I doing wrong?" "Why am I still broken?" "Why can't I fix this?" It brought up a lot of shame, having people look at my hands and ask if I had been burned.

It also brought up a lot of doubt. I felt like I should be able to solve the problem with all the healing tools I'd learned. Even though I don't help my clients with physical ailments, I do a lot of work around mindset, and it didn't feel like I was acing the test in this situation. My hands felt linked to my emotions, so my ego kept telling me that I didn't know what I was doing, that I didn't have powerful enough tools, if I had this huge rash sticking around.

For months, I'd tried everything I could think of. Doctors simply suggested the same things I'd already tried. I began exploring many different Eastern healing modalities. I was monitoring my reactions to foods, my stress, my emotions, my workout routine—and none of it worked.

During one of my shamanic journeys, my teacher suggested I journey to my hands in order to ask what the eczema wanted to say to me. Why it might be showing up. The message I kept getting was, "You've pushed down so much for so long. So many emotions. So many fears. And now your body is finally out of fight or flight mode. It's finally safe to release. And you can't hurry that. You're doing everything. Keep going."

At first that message was really reassuring. I was doing the right things. And it absolutely felt true that my body needed to release all sorts of sadness, anger, anxiousness, and fear that I had pushed to the side in an attempt to be strong and get stuff done.

So I kept unpacking the moments of emotion still stored in my body. I kept up with the diet and the workouts. My stress, on average, felt lower than it had been in a while.

The progress on my hands? Still minimal. Slightly better at best. That was even more frustrating. Eventually, I got tired of talking about it. Tired of friends asking how it was. Tired of thinking about it.

And I surrendered.

Coming from a past of severe anxiety, that wasn't something that was easy for me. I'd always been worried about worst case scenarios. Always trying to have plan A, and then plans B-Z in case the first plan didn't quite work out. I was desperately trying to control the world around me because I didn't feel safe. I didn't feel grounded. I was afraid the good things in my life were slipping away.

That's where I needed personal development and spirituality, to heal some of those deep-rooted wounds. The most beautiful peace in my life has come from surrender. Surrender is necessary for growth. We surrender over and over again to doing the scary, stretchy things.

When I first started my business, it was terrifying to try on the clothes of a coach, so to speak. I didn't know if I was doing it right. I worried all the time about being good enough. As my business evolved, it was nerve-wracking to add in new ways of helping people, new tools I hadn't practiced as many times. What got me through was surrendering to where my soul was leading me. It wasn't by accident that my clients came into my world. It wasn't by accident that we got on a call. And it wasn't by accident that they said yes to working with me.

I surrendered to what the Universe was putting into my path, and to the belief that if an opportunity is showing up for me, then I'm ready for it.

Some simple affirmations were deeply helpful as I moved into that place of trust. Things like:

"I am safe, protected, and fully provided for."

"I allow it to get even better."

"I trust that it's always working out for the greatest good."

"It's always perfect."

And when things were working out in amazing ways:

"This, or something better, is coming my way"

Writing or speaking these affirmations alone didn't

## Chapter 23: Keep Expanding Your Toolkit

change my life. I had to believe them. I had to feel them in my body, and know they were true.

That's the journey. That's the growth. That's why I work with healers and coaches, and have deep practices in my daily life. Because we are constantly releasing old stories, releasing what society tells us, and releasing pain from past lives or those around us. It's a journey we say yes to, again and again.

As I kept surrendering to the situation with my hands, one of my teachers said, "What if you stopped trying to fix it?"

And so I did.

Truthfully, I'm still on a journey with it. I wish I could say that as of writing this, it's all gone and it's all good! I can say that it's so much better than it has been. I can say that it has led me to healing modalities and healing moments that I am beyond grateful for.

The process I've been through to heal my hands led me to tools, ceremonies, and processes I use with my clients every single week. I needed to go through that process to become the leader I was meant to be. My brain needed a reason to explore that world, so the Universe gave it to me.

Take a moment to think about where your pain might be leading you. It could be something that happened in the past, or something still coming up in this moment. When you ask your soul, and your heart, what the situation is here to teach, what do you hear? What comes up? How can you start to understand where the Universe is leading you?

CHAPTER 24

# Don't Be Surprised If Resistance Shows Up

*I* think too often we picture our "soul path" and our "purpose" as coming to us in one sweeping moment when everything magically works out. Here's the thing: a lot of doors will open when you say yes. The Universe will absolutely make magic happen that you never imagined. You'll feel more fulfilled and happier than you've ever been. But not every moment will feel magical, happy, and easy.

Saying yes to your soul requires courage. It means being willing to face challenges because it's for your greatest good, and it's a lesson you need to learn to help others. It means getting uncomfortable and stretching your comfort zone every single day.

Even with the anxiety I faced growing up, I signed up for debate class. In college, I took on leadership roles.

Once I graduated college and got a job, I ran important client meetings. When I launched my business, I started showing up on video with no makeup and in my workout clothes.

Even though it made no sense at the time, I would say, "I just really feel like I need to...I need to so I can do what I want to later in life."

Ultimately, my fears could have turned into resistance if I had let them. The insecurities I had could've been great reasons to stop trying. The fears showed up in some pretty intense ways, but part of me always knew that I was meant for more.

It feels appropriate to write this chapter on resistance right now. Because when sitting down to write today, I saw resistance show up in so many different ways: body aches, feeling incredibly tired, hunger, feeling uninspired, feeling unclear, unmotivated, or like I don't know what to say, and working on other things instead of this book (because of course my clients have a bunch of questions!).

I had the thoughts, "I don't feel like it" and "I need to be in the right mood/mindset to do this."

It's funny because so much of the advice out there is to follow your excitement, to take action when you feel high-vibe. But if you make that your rule, resistance will come in the form of you feeling unclear, and simply a little off. It becomes easy to procrastinate, to say you'll feel better tomorrow.

Right now, resistance means me staring at the page and considering whether to delete every single word I've written.

## Chapter 24: Don't Be Surprised If Resistance Shows Up

I'm human. So are you, so resistance is going to come up every now and then.

That's why I strongly believe in understanding your soul's mission and in doing the work to understand why you're on this path is so important. There are days when it doesn't feel fun. There are days when you're not sure if it's worth it, if you're actually meant for this work, if you're doing any of it right.

What gets me through is tuning in to my heart and remembering all the things that got me here. Maybe it's the version of me five years ago, the one miserable at a corporate job and waiting for five minutes of freedom on a walk around the block. Maybe it's the version of me starting a business, who took a big leap and was figuring out how to make it work. Who was healing on the go, moving through a lifetime of labels and fears while getting her shit together to pay rent at the end of the month. Maybe it's for the version of me who continued saying yes, continued pushing through the fear, the doubts, the worry, because there was a small voice inside saying, "It just feels right." I call on these versions of me. I call on these voices. They are why I don't walk away.

If there's a part of you who knows you're meant to help people, meant to make an impact, and meant to do something bigger, then tap into that fire. Find a way to hold hands with your fear and your resistance, and do it anyway.

Take a moment to call out some forms of resistance you've seen show up for you in the past. It might be getting a cold right before a big event is meant to happen. It might be prioritizing other things (the dishes always seem to be my favorite) so that all of a sudden there isn't time for the thing you're meant to do. It might be always saying "I don't know" instead of diving deeper and really finding the answers in your journal or in meditation.

Resistance can be tricky, so know that how it shows up may change from time to time. That's why this part of the work is deeply important. Awareness is key to choosing differently.

*Some days I want to scream,*

*Do you even want it?!*

*The thing you say you crave*

*The business. The freedom. The travel. The relationship.*

*Because you have to do things differently.*

*You have to try.*

*No one else can make it happen.*

*Why is it so easy to dream, but can feel so hard to do?*

*What breaks my heart…*

*All that's holding you back is knowing you're worth it.*

*And I see the beauty. The power. The talent in you.*

*So what will it take?*

*For you to see it,*

*To believe it,*

*To choose this different version of you.*

*That you have to declare can exist.*

CHAPTER 25

# The Universe Is on Your Side

As you get more ideas and more visions, it's extremely common to feel overwhelmed. Many of my clients start to see ways they are meant to help, to heal, and to serve that feel insanely out of reach.

This happened to me when, a couple of months into launching my business, I had a sudden and huge realization. One of the visions of what I was meant to create had come to me years earlier—far before I had any idea what it really was, far before I knew I wanted a business. As long ago as when I was in college, I could picture a beautiful forest with amazing energy. It felt like love and celebration. I had absolutely no idea what I was seeing or where it was, but I did mentally agree that I'd go to that place when I figured out where it was.

When I started doing PR and event planning, the vision came to me again. At that point, I felt like I was onto the message: I'm meant to create and organize that space for someone else! Got it. On it. As soon as I knew who wanted an event like that, I'd be their right hand.

Then, once I started my coaching business and working with clients, it hit me over the head. I was meant to create that space. I was meant to hold retreats.

Man, that was way more terrifying.

The vision had to come to me in steps. No part of me would've been ready for the whole message back in college. I didn't even know I wanted a business, much less think I was capable of running my own event.

It's my deep belief that we all are capable of much more than we know, and the only reason we don't have the full picture is because our brains kick it out. We would laugh it off even if we saw it.

That's why it's so important to keep taking steps forward with what you know. Once I understood the retreat vision was actually for me to create, I knew the Universe was serious about how magical that space was meant to be. You don't have visions coming to you for five years unless there's a truly divine reason.

Just to be clear, even once I knew what I was supposed to do, I didn't make it happen overnight. I had a lot of fear come up. I was only about six months into running my business full time, and had no idea if people would come to an event. I was terrified at the idea of standing in front of a big table meant to be filled with people, but only having one or two show up.

The good news was, at this point, I'd learned to surrender to the nudges. I'd seen time and time again how my fear hadn't stopped the Universe from moving its plans forward. It just caused resistance and pain if I tried to dig my heels in. So I made a list of what scared me most. Some were thoughts and worries, and some were logistical. The list got long. Then, I separated it into what I could control, and what I had to surrender to the Universe. For example, there's no way I could control the weather. But worrying about where the event would be held, that was something that could be worked out.

This led to one of my favorite practices: bargaining with the Universe. It works better than you might think.

I wrote a letter to the Universe explaining everything I was feeling: The vision I'd had. All the fears that came up. Why I knew I was meant to hold this event. Everything that felt like it was in my way.

Since the venue was one of the biggest obstacles for me, I started there. I'm pretty sure the sentence I wrote went something like, "I know you want me to have this event. And I'm up for whatever I'm meant to do to serve. So, if I'm really meant to do this, I need your help. I'm really stressed about where to hold this event since it doesn't feel right to host a group of people in my small studio apartment. Can you please show me where? Somewhere that is close by, that comes to me easily, that just feels right. If you give me a place, I'll take it as a sign and make the rest happen. I just need your help with this one."

Even as I wrote that, for this book, my word count ended in "555," a magical number. The Universe is truly listening, I promise.

So what happened? In less than a month, I was

shown the perfect space. Through a personal development group, I was introduced to an amazing woman and I friended her on Facebook. Right as the friend request was accepted, I saw her latest post. She had just launched a Facebook page for her property, a retreat site in the redwoods less than two hours away from where I lived.

Close. Magical. Easy.

I started laughing. And actually whispered the words, "I'm on it" to the Universe.

I'll never forget this moment. It was a reminder to me that we aren't alone in making our goals happen. As much as our brains want to figure it all out, there's so much help we can ask for. When you're moving forward your soul's mission and doing the work you're meant to on this Earth, the Universe wants to help you. You have team members: your soul, your angels, your guides, and even the people around you. So stop holding all the weight. Ask for what you need. It's amazing how the Universe responds.

Try it for yourself. Write out what you know of your vision and how you'd love help from the Universe. What can you acknowledge is meant for you to do and create, and what are the parts you need to collaborate with the Universe to make happen?

CHAPTER 26

# That Time I Called in All the Ancestors

There's no way I can go into all the amazing, crazy, powerful healing moments I've had (the book would be huge, and it wouldn't actually help you get closer to your goals, your healing, and your truth). Yet, I do need to share a bit more. When I say that you don't need to be fully healed to start helping others, I know that, while it sounds good in theory, your brain might not love it. So I want to share an example of how the Universe continually gave me exactly what I needed to heal, to up-level, and to keep helping my clients on a deeper level, even when my brain had no idea what that meant or what I really needed. One of the biggest things I've learned is that starting on the path of healing leads you to new levels, to new depths, and to new modalities—especially when you keep moving forward with an open heart and the intention to honor your soul's path and soul's mission.

That's how I somehow ended up at a business retreat in Tulum, in a sweat lodge, in some of the most extreme pain I've ever been in.

But let me back up.

At that point, my soul had already led me to shamanic healing. I'd been deep in the process of healing my relationship with my dad, and watching for signs and messages from him. My business was thriving, and I was hitting goals that I thought would take five or ten years to accomplish.

For a few months prior to the sweat lodge, I felt big lessons bubbling up to be seen and heard. Things around self-worth. Self-love. Why the traumas in my life happened. And finally, for the first time since I was eight, I was trying to calm my nervous system so I didn't constantly feel like the bottom could drop out at any time.

I knew some major healing was going to happen in Tulum. But technically it was a business retreat…so I kept an open mind about where that expectation was coming from.

There were a lot of reasons Tulum held major healing for me. It started with butterflies, which I consider my sign from the Universe, showing up everywhere. They were constantly surrounding me. Sometimes it was just one or two on the path nearby, but other times it was hundreds flying over the house. My coach even said, "Where's Sarah?! I know she's around…it looks like someone set an entire butterfly house free."

## Chapter 26: That Time I Called in All the Ancestors

There definitely was a magic to Tulum. We went to see the Mayan ruins, and I could feel the energy change as we approached. We biked around the grounds, and spent lots of time stopping to soak in the energy, from the ruins to the trees. We then had the chance to climb up one of the pyramids. We were invited by our guide to do this barefoot, to truly soak in the experience. But there was another reason to be barefoot—it was insanely steep! There was a rope up the middle that you could hold onto, but otherwise there was nothing but uneven and even sometimes crumbling stone steps with no railing. The best way up was to only look at the step in front of you, and to never look down. It was constantly just about getting your feet grounded on the next step, slowly but surely. What an amazing metaphor for life.

At the top, you were high above the trees. It felt like you could double the height of the tallest tree, and it still wouldn't touch the top of this pyramid. Most other people were wandering around, but as soon as I got to the top I felt an overwhelming amount of emotion. Maybe it was fear from climbing up. Maybe it was gratitude. There wasn't really a thought, just so many tears. I sat on the side of the pyramid, staring at one of the trees that had grown off the side. I just sat there, releasing so much. The interesting thing is that I felt light, loving, and powerful energy all around me. It was almost too much to take in.

We were supposed to walk, observing the area around us, but I just sat and cried. It was hard to put words to. It was just an immense feeling when I tuned in to the energy. The biggest thought I had was that it was interesting to see that it felt hard to let in the lightness. That so much had to be pushed out to let it in.

When our group started heading down, I was one of the last ones off the top. I ended up crab-walking my way down—partially because it was easier, and partially because my hands wanted to be on the stones as much as possible. We kept biking through the ruins, and after we returned our bikes I was told that a white butterfly had been following me the whole time.

We jumped back into the car, and weren't told where our next destination was. Eventually we hopped out, and were told to be in our swimsuits and shower off. After walking down a steep staircase we emerged into a cave with a giant pool of water in the middle—a cenote. Traditionally, this was known as the closest to the underworld you can get. It was gorgeous, with beautiful stalactites hanging down. We jumped into the water, and it was freezing. It was hard to catch my breath. The water was so dark I had no clue what was under me. A rock could have been inches away, about to hit my foot, or it could have been an incredibly far distance between me and the bottom. We were able to swim in a circle though the cenote, going under low edges of the cave and over some rocks sticking high up in the water. The energy felt heavy, dark, cold, and slow. It was an amazing contrast to the Mayan ruins.

What I found the most interesting was how much easier my body handled being in the darkness, in what was considered "heavy energy," versus in the light. It almost felt natural, like my body knew how to handle it, compared

## Chapter 26: That Time I Called in All the Ancestors

to all the tears that came up on the top of the Mayan ruins. That led to some big thoughts: What if we are just accustomed to struggle? What if we are constantly swimming in these deep, heavy emotions, when there is lightness just waiting for us when we step outside of the water?

I had to sit with that one for a while. It might resonate with you as well. Have you been making it harder than you need to, when lightness is just waiting for you in a place not too far away?

You might think that was more than enough magic for one retreat. But I haven't even gotten to where I started this story: the sweat lodge. This was meant to be another surprise, and we found out the day before. The moment I found out, my body felt crazy heavy. At the time I ignored it—nerves, right? It's new. Unknown.

But then it was the day of. We were hours before leaving, and my head felt fine. My thoughts weren't going crazy, which was surprising. Usually my head is filled with worries like, "What's going to happen? Am I going to get tired? What if it's too hot? What if I can't handle it?"

Instead, my head was quiet, knowing everything would be okay. But from my neck down, I was freaking out. I felt anxious. Nauseous. And I was bawling my eyes out. With zero input from my thoughts. I've truly never felt anything like it. Usually I notice my body is responding to my thoughts. And this time felt totally, completely different.

The group noticed how much I was going through and kept reminding me I had a choice. I could stay at the villa. I didn't have to go.

I decided to get in the car and go to the location, to see how my body felt.

On getting there, my body did calm down a little. It almost felt like it surrendered, and was ready to go with the flow. The smells of the plants felt like home, and it was incredibly soothing to be on the Earth, in the mud.

There are some parts of the lodge that I won't write about. It felt like a sacred space that wasn't meant for all eyes. But there was a part of my experience I need to share.

In the beginning, we were asked to call in any ancestors or guides we felt called to. I called in my dad, who, as I mentioned, I'd been doing major healing around. My intention was to release his pain, from him and me, so we both could be free.

Then I called in my mom's ancestral line, to heal any pain that was still being held onto. At the time, I thought that was normal. It was just what I felt called to do. I later learned...that's a lot. Like, a big undertaking.

So, how did it go? The first half was certainly hot. A lot of emotions and fears came up, but the experience was along the lines of what I'd expected.

The second half? I started to feel like I needed to lie down, and I did. I felt every part of my body touching that dirt floor. I felt like I needed to get grounded, so I started to dig my hands in the dirt underneath us. Then, I noticed that my hands had started forming themselves into claws. No matter what I did to release them, they wouldn't open.

I started to panic and try to force them to relax. What did this mean? What was happening? The more I tried to

## Chapter 26: That Time I Called in All the Ancestors

force them open, the more painful they got. They were clenching tighter, and there truly wasn't anything I could do about it.

At that point, it became all about calming my mind. I had to fully surrender, to believe I was fine, to tell myself this was meant to happen. I kept digging my hands into the earth, because it was the only thing that made them feel better.

I have no idea if we were there for five minutes or five hours, but my mind was certainly elsewhere. I remember our guide calling us to put our hand on our heart, and I felt frustrated because I couldn't. I just had a claw.

Eventually the sweat lodge ceremony concluded. Everyone made their way out, but I couldn't move my body. There was energy pulsing. My hands were hurting. I didn't think I could stand up.

I lay in the empty tent for a long time. Eventually a voice in me said, "You have to move. They're worried. Just try to get out."

I wasn't certain I could. I crawled, on hands and knees, to the edge. The second I made it out the door, I collapsed on the ground. Just getting that far had taken every bit of energy I had. I then heard the woman leading us say, "Go over to the mat, like the princess you are!"

I didn't feel like a princess at all. I felt wrung out, completely limp. I laughed in my head at the idea of being royal or regal in that moment, and even at the idea of trying to move at all. Somehow I managed to crawl over to the mat and dig my hands back into the dirt nearby. They were still clenched, still not moving.

She came by with tea, which my hands could only hold in claw form. As I sipped the tea, I dug my hands back into the earth. Slowly, they started to loosen. My thumbs had never felt so sore. I lay on my back feeling the pain and energy pulse through me.

She called upon the group, and one by one, everyone discussed their experience. I didn't want to talk. I had no words yet. But I could feel the energy of the group, and knew they were wondering what happened. I managed to choke out the words, "I'm still… processing. But that was painful. One of the most painful things I've ever experienced."

From the other side of the group, I heard a voice: "I'm so glad she spoke! I was so worried!" I later learned that when I crawled out of the tent, a few of the women there were worried I wasn't okay. They asked the guide, and she said, "Sarah's deadddddd…it's good!"

She was right. Some big parts of the old Sarah died in there. I was able to leave behind some of the fears and the pain. I was able to surrender at a deeper level than I ever had before, and trust in whatever was happening in that moment, no matter how painful it was.

You might be wondering how all this impacted my eczema. My skin condition actually didn't change a ton. It was better right after that day and then, in some ways, got worse. Looking back on those moments in the sweat lodge, my gut feeling is that even more energy started releasing from my body in ways I didn't know I needed. Digging into the earth absolutely felt like grounding, since there was so much energy moving, and my hands desperately needed to feel safe and secure and connected to the Earth. Why my hands are so significant is a question that seems to be still unfolding. I do sense it's symbolic of my work as a healer. It's a constant reminder to deepen my own healing, and stay in balance between giving to others and healing myself.

Even as I type this, my thumbs feel sore. I can still feel all that energy, everything that was released. It's a reminder to me of how much we carry. Why this work is so important. And crawling out of the tent took fighting. It took will power. It took determination. It took choosing to move when it didn't feel good.

You are being led to exactly what you need for the next version of you to emerge. It certainly doesn't need to be in a sweat lodge or in a foreign country. You get to keep saying yes to the healing, yes to the signs, and yes to healing yourself and healing others. There's a depth to the work you're doing that your brain can't understand.

If you were to picture the re-born version of you, the most authentic version of you that's ready to come out, what comes up? What version of you is being created in this exact moment? Notice what that version of you looks like, feels like, and is doing. Also, write out what feels like the next step in your healing to get there. What needs to be seen, loved, and given attention? Remember, whatever comes up is perfect. It's never by accident.

CHAPTER 27

# Are You Appreciating the Mountain?

In going through this process, you might feel like you're endlessly peeling back layers of the onion. There are times you'll feel like superwoman, like you've got it all handled and the Universe is on your side, making it happen. There will also be times you feel confused, lost, and discouraged. I'm not going to sugarcoat that.

There are three really important things that can help you make it through those times. The first is having an amazing coach or healer in your corner. I can't stress enough that, as my business grew, my self-care deepened and my support team grew. You'll need someone who understands how resistance shows up for you, what your soul goals are, and how to nurture you through those moments where every part of your brain wants to walk away.

The second thing is visualizing the future moments that will mean so much to you. For me, it was always picturing the messages from clients saying how much I helped change their lives. I thought of them saying things like, "That's exactly what I needed to hear," and, "Truly, I can't even express what a light you are in my life." The reality is, the wins are even bigger than that. I still tear up when I think about it.

Here are some words from a client that make my heart sing:

> *"This is for the woman who just got home from the job that sucks the soul right outta her. She has some sort of side hustle or creative outlet that keeps getting the back burner because she just can't balance it all and she's BURNING tf OUT. I want you to know you're getting that nudge to pursue that dream on purpose, it's hitting you right on time, and you HAVE TO FOLLOW IT girl!!*
>
> *I took the leap of faith from my 9-5 in September of last year after getting the soul tap \*so loud\* that I needed to put all of my energy into building my online coaching (my side gig at the time). It made ZERO sense for me to leap when I did (I didn't have a single paying client, no real business plan or idea of what the hell I was actually going to do, no money saved up AND I had debt) but I listened anyway.*
>
> *I put in a LOT OF WORK. I hired a coach to help me navigate this wild ride. I got super clear on what my dream life will look like, and made it my mission to get myself there.*

## Chapter 27: Are You Appreciating the Mountain?

*I went deep into what my blocks were. What beliefs were holding me back. I exercised the hell out of my intuition muscles, and learned how to hear the messages my soul was sending me about what to do next. Perhaps most importantly, I leaned HARD into two of the biggest game changers I've ever experienced: TRUST and SURRENDER. I gave it up to God and the Universe to use me as a vessel and lead me to what I was meant to be doing.*

*Flash forward to today: I am officially completely and comfortably supporting myself financially from my own coaching biz. I am currently BOOKED OUT working with a full client load of the EXACT description of my "dream client" I wrote out earlier this year. I am seriously obsessed with everyone I am working with right now and have cried from gratitude on a regular basis because they light my freakin' soul on fire. It feels so. fooking. good.*

*I'm pretty sure I personally \*experienced\* all of the fears that hold people back from doing this kind of thing, and it was uncomfortable, yes, but HOLY CRAP was it necessary, and holy SH%& was it worth it."*

I share this to say: it gets better than your brain can even imagine.

The third way to keep yourself going is to step back now and again to appreciate how far you've come. This growth process happens fast, and if you take your next steps seriously, you could be at a point where you have paying clients within just a couple months. All of a sudden your goals will go from "figure out what I want to do next" to "have three paying clients" to "hit 10K months." With each step forward, it's valuable and needed to reflect and give yourself credit for how far you've come. Otherwise, you'll find it all too easy to be hard on yourself and think you aren't reaching your goals fast enough. When you're climbing the mountain, you need to stop and appreciate how amazing it is that you've gotten this high.

*What's the part of you that you're trying to hide?*
*The fact that would ruin you.*
*The story that terrifies you.*
*The one you keep covered up, in a sealed box in your mind.*
*That's your power.*
*That's the part of you that needs to be set free.*
*Let it see the light of day.*
*And that light,*
*The first rays of sunlight*
*Get to be your love.*

CHAPTER 28

# Your Dreams Are Not an Experiment

As much as this whole book is about exploring and understanding the next steps meant for you on this journey, I want to end with a reminder that your dreams are not an experiment. There are lots of variables and lots of potential outcomes, and it's your job to keep moving forward

The second you take away the thought "Is this going to work?" and replace it with the knowledge that things are always working out and that you can always adjust and figure it out, that's when deep trust comes in.

The things that make you happy shouldn't just be a priority when it's convenient. It may sound like common sense, but when things get difficult, how quickly are you willing to compromise on what you want? On what you truly deserve?

It's a choice to pick comfort versus a challenge or a new direction. The path that's calling to you might require more work, more discomfort, and more dedication, but there's still a reason it's calling to you.

How are you treating yourself when you stay quiet because others might think you're crazy? How are you treating yourself when you don't take your goals seriously and let things get in the way?

Writing in the sun was always my dream. Something I pictured when I was a little kid, imagining my dream life. Writing in the sun, walking on the beach, learning and growing, and seriously impacting other people. The moments are so meaningful because they're what I always wanted—but wasn't letting in.

I imagined this perfect day when I was super little. So what happened? Why did it take a couple of decades for me to experience the pure bliss of living my dream?

I chose other things. I chose making other people happy. Stability. Security. Making continual, small compromises because it still seemed "good enough." Truthfully, I was prioritizing other values over my happiness. And it took a major transformation to find my way back to myself.

As kids, our instinct was to choose happiness. We wanted ice cream for dinner, to stay up way too late, to roll down grassy hills, and to confidently ask for a second sticker when we were only offered one. Then the world started to label things good and bad.

As an adult, we need to actively tell ourselves, "I am worth it."

## Chapter 28: Your Dreams Are Not an Experiment

We need to decide: "I am picking alignment. I am choosing happiness. I am prioritizing my own dream."

Choosing that path led me to writing parts of this book while staring out over the ocean, with the sun shining down on my head and the breeze in my hair. I'm so grateful to say my heart found what it was searching for. It was inside me all along, and just needed my permission to be set free.

Now it's your turn.

# Acknowledgments

It's a little overwhelming to know where to start when I think of the list of people who deserve a shout-out in this book.

First, to every single one of my clients. As much as I've helped you along our journey, you have been the inspiration along mine. You take this whole thing from a concept into reality. You are the ones showing up and doing such big work in the world, and it's truly an honor to be part of your journey. Without knowing it, so many of you have been the fire in my belly, and the light that keeps me going when things get hard. Thinking of the leaps you've made, the things you've created, and the way your lives have changed is what makes it all worth it.

To my husband, Charlie, who has been by my side for so much of this journey. As I'm writing this book, we've been together for ten years and counting. I said it in my vows, and I'll say it again now. I'm so grateful the Universe gave me you so early in life. You've supported me, challenged me, pushed me, and ultimately been a key part of so much of my growth. I'm so grateful for your willingness to explore the world, and life, with me.

To my mom! You always would say you planted the seeds, and I can't agree more. You nurtured me into who I am today. You showed strength during some of the most challenging times in our life, and truly were a superwoman of a mother. I know you don't give yourself enough credit for how amazing you are, so I want to do it in this somewhat public way. I'm honored to have you as my mom. I think you are one of the strongest, most loving, most intelligent people I know, and I'm so grateful for the way you raised me, and for the conversations about angels and energy and healing that we get to have now.

To my dad—I know he won't ever get to read this, but his spirit will. His spirit has been here through so much of this. Dad, you have so many good traits that I'm so insanely proud to embody. Your entrepreneurship, your tenacity, your deep desire to help others…it's all in me, and in this book. Thank you for being my guide.

To my powerful, badass business coach, Steph Gold. You've seen parts of me that almost no one else has. Thank you for creating a beautiful, powerful, safe space that has helped me grow in more ways than I can count. I'm grateful that you saw me, and my potential, even when I wasn't that clear on it. Thank you for every moment of love, of belief, of motivation, and of magic that you've poured into me. I know you've gone above and beyond in so many ways, and I'm so deeply grateful.

To Caity, my beautiful shamanic teacher! Thank you

## Acknowledgments

for being such a powerful guide. You unlocked such deep healing for me around my feminine side and my connection to spirit. You truly unlocked magic that continues to unfold.

To Lindsay, for the magical retreat in Costa Rica that I mention in this book. You are my mermaid, witch, and forest fairy soul sister, and I'm so grateful to have you in my life!

To Elisa Romeo, author of *Meet Your Soul,* your book and your medicine unlocked so much on this journey. Thank you for helping me build a relationship with my soul when I needed to most.

To Sanne, for being so willing to give me time and love so early in this entrepreneurial journey. Our conversation in that coffee shop ignited sparks that truly turned into such brilliant light for others. Thank you for your kind heart, your wisdom, and seeing me.

To Peta Kelly, for creating the Supercharged community. You created a group of women who have changed my life. Your community was the first public place I went after my dad passed away, and is where my entrepreneur spark was nourished in so many ways. Thank you for honoring your soul and your truth, and for creating such powerful containers.

To Maggie, my badass editor, who helped make sure this book happened. Writing a book is big work, and I'm so grateful for your help in making sure it came into the world in as beautiful a form as possible.

And there are so many more of you, you know who you are, who have been so important to me on this journey. My soul sisters and brothers who have seen me, poured love into me, and been essential to where I am today. If we've crossed paths, you've made a difference. I'm so grateful for all the divine connections in this life.

# Resources

Below is a list of some books and teachers I've learned from in such deep ways and who inevitably influenced the content of this book. This list is constantly growing and evolving, but this is a place to start!

*Meet Your Soul* by Elisa Romeo

*The Earth Is Hiring* by Peta Kelly

*The Alchemist* by Paulo Coelho

*The Artist's Way* by Julia Cameron

*Big Magic* by Elizabeth Gilbert

*The Big Leap* by Gay Hendricks

*You Can Heal Your Life* by Louis Hay

*The Four Agreements* by Don Miguel Ruiz

# About the Author

*SARAH KLEINER*

Sarah Kleiner works with women who are starting to build their own businesses, helping them get clear on what their souls are here to do and to become lighthouses for the things they want to attract. She has a marketing and PR background, where she did work ranging from crisis communications for a Fortune 500 company to branding, content, and PR for startups. She combines this with extensive training in coaching, herbalism, and shamanic and somatic practices to help people step into their authentic self and build the life they've been craving. She lives in San Francisco with her husband Charlie and her two cat sidekicks, Molly and Milo. Learn more at www.sarahkleiner.com.

# Just For You!

My number one goal with this book is to make an impact, and by reading this you're making that dream possible. To make sure you have everything you need, I created a workbook that will help you get clarity on what you're meant to create, as well as your aligned next steps. The workbook includes all the questions and exercises mentioned throughout the book, so you can do them at your own pace, as well as some bonuses that will keep your energy moving! You can download it at www.sarahkleiner.com/soulnudge.

Along with the workbook, I also keep time open in my calendar for virtual coffee chats as a way of paying forward all the time and energy that was poured into me at the beginning of my journey. Visit www.teawithsarah.com to schedule a time to connect.

www.ingramcontent.com/pod-product-compliance
Lightning Source LLC
Chambersburg PA
CBHW021407290426
44108CB00010B/429